ICE BOWL '67

THE PACKERS, THE COWBOYS, AND THE GAME THAT CHANGED THE NFL

CHUCK CARLSON

FOREWORD BY DAN REEVES

SPORTS
PUBLISHING

Sports Publishing books may be purchased in bulk at special discounts for sales promotion, corporate gifts, fund-raising, or educational purposes. Special editions can also be created to specifications. For details, contact the Special Sales Department, Sports Publishing, 307 West 36th Street, 11th Floor, New York, NY 10018 or sportspubbooks@skyhorsepublishing.com.

Sports Publishing® is a registered trademark of Skyhorse Publishing, Inc.®, a Delaware corporation.

Visit our website at www.sportspubbooks.com.

10 9 8 7 6 5 4 3 2 1

Library of Congress Cataloging-in-Publication Data is available on file.

Cover design by Tom Lau
Cover photo credit: Associated Press

All photos in the insert courtesy of Associated Press

ISBN: 978-1-68358-097-3
Ebook ISBN: 978-1-68358-101-7

Printed in the United States of America

CONTENTS

ACKNOWLEDGMENTS

DO A SIMPLE Google search on the term *Ice Bowl* and prepare to be amazed. Thanks to the wonderful world of digital technology where no information is too far away, more than three million results will be available to you in less than a second. And that's just "Ice Bowl" too. Not "Green Bay Packers and Ice Bowl" or "Dallas Cowboys and Ice Bowl" or "NFL and Ice Bowl" or "Tom Landry and Ice Bowl." You can fill the Lambeau Field stands with all the results of a game played before a fair portion of the population of the United States was even born.

Everybody, it seems, has written or commented or viewed or analyzed what remains the most famous, and infamous game, in NFL history. And it was fifty years ago.

Just think about that for a moment. Fifty years later and that football game continues to hold sway. And why not?

There have been books, TV specials, magazine articles, newspaper analyses, blogs, and personal remembrances written about the game played between the Green Bay Packers and Dallas Cowboys on December 31, 1967, when the greatest foe was not the opposing team but the elements.

The stories would flow, and still flow, from those who played and watched what is still considered the NFL's most memorable contest.

Yes, there were candidates before and after the Packers and Cowboys played each other on that crystalline Sunday afternoon.

Only nine years earlier, the Baltimore Colts had beaten the New York Giants when running back Alan Ameche smashed into the end zone at Yankee Stadium to carve out a rugged 23–17 overtime win that sealed the NFL championship and was dubbed by the hyperbolic media of the day the "greatest game ever played."

There were games that followed, such as the incredible Pittsburgh Steelers victory in the AFC playoffs over the Oakland Raiders in 1972 when Franco Harris plucked a seemingly incomplete pass off his shoetops for the game-winning score.

Or the 1981 season classic when the San Diego Chargers, exhausted and battered, held off the Miami Dolphins in an AFC divisional playoff win.

There have been other games that toyed with the title of the greatest ever but soon were seen as lacking, at least when placed in comparison to the 1967 battle in Green Bay.

True, pro football's two best teams were also playing each other that afternoon and had the weather been simply Wisconsin-in-the-middle-of-winter cold, it might have been, it should have been, a classic. But sometime overnight, the rules changed and Wisconsin cold became Antarctic cold and winning took on a whole different meaning.

And what should have been a classic became immortal.

It was a game that has settled into the American sporting psyche and has not been dislodged to this day. And when another football game is played in cold weather, the references to the "Ice Bowl" flow back as a reference point and source of pride.

But there was only one Ice Bowl, and everyone, all these years later, knows it.

Interestingly enough, in researching this book, those who took part in the event never seem to tire of talking about it. They can still see a frozen Lambeau Field and recall how taking a deep breath was like a knife in their lungs and how they were beaten up physically, emotionally and every other way a football player could be tested.

They still remember everything about that game because, even as they played it, they knew they were part of something special.

So I wish to thank the players from both the Packers and Cowboys, most of them happily ensconced in retirement and someplace warm, for taking time to, yet again, relive the game that needs no introduction.

As well, I'd like to acknowledge the work of three other books that brought the Ice Bowl back to life—*Ice Bowl: The Cold Truth About Football's Most Unforgettable Game* by Ed Gruver; *The Ice Bowl: The Green Bay Packers and Dallas Cowboys Season of 1967* by Mike Shropshire, and David Maraniss's peerless biography of Vince Lombardi, *When Still Pride Mattered.*

Obviously, much has been written about the game and the men who played in it. But even all these decades later, there is always something more to learn, something more to analyze, something more to reveal.

But even with all the words that have been written about it, they can never tell the whole story. The fifty years that have followed have made icons of players such as Jerry Kramer, Bart Starr, Dan Reeves, Chuck Mercein, and Don Meredith.

Some have told their stories time and again, happy to relive it. Others have not. And maybe that's because the re-telling can never capture what truly happened.

Those memories are stored away, safe from prying eyes and misunderstandings.

And, perhaps, maybe that's the way it should be.

FOREWORD

STARTING IN 1981, I had the privilege of being a head coach in the National Football League. I coached the Denver Broncos for 13 seasons, helping take them to three Super Bowls. I coached four seasons for the New York Giants, and then I concluded my coaching career with the Atlanta Falcons, returning to the Super Bowl in 1999.

Before that, I played and was an assistant coach for the Dallas Cowboys.

And along the way, I was part of many memorable games and had the good fortune to coach and watch more great players than I can name.

But it's a game I was involved in fifty years ago that people still ask me about all the time, maybe more than any other. They want to know what it was like and what I remember about the

ICE BOWL '67

NFL Championship Game played on December 31, 1967 in Green Bay, Wisconsin.

It became known as the "Ice Bowl" and it has become a part of pro football history and, I suppose, a part of American history, too. No one who played in that game thought about that at the time—I know I didn't. But as the years have gone by, the significance of that game, and everything that went with it, has become clear.

We have watched replays of the games on TV over the years. We have replayed it in our minds. We remembered, as we walked outside for the first time that Sunday morning, that none of us, on either team, had been as cold as were then and we never would be again. And more than a few of us wondered if it was insanity to play football in that kind of weather.

But we did and both the Packers and Cowboys produced a game that would never be forgotten.

So when people ask me about the Ice Bowl, I'm always happy to answer because I've learned it was much more than a football game. It was about survival and perseverance and making the best of a bad situation, and that was another lesson those of us involved didn't understand at the time but eventually would.

And when fans want to know how and why we played a game everyone still looks at as the coldest game ever played, I find those are easy questions to answer. We did it because that's what we did. And how did we do it? Who knows? Instinct takes over. So did competitiveness. The will to win overrides everything including frozen fields and fingers in those situations. Winning anytime is great, but winning when everything is going against you, how much better is that?

So we played the best we could under the circumstances. And maybe that's why the Ice Bowl is still so fondly remembered. Football, even in the best circumstances, is a tough game played by tough men. But when you can't feel your hands or your feet, and when you hit the turf and it feels like you landed on a sheet of ice, even tough men begin to think twice.

As a player or coach, I have never been a part of anything like the Ice Bowl. It was a strange combination of odd circumstances and incredible individual performances that made a game that, very likely, will never be seen again.

It was more than the Green Bay Packers, the established but aging NFL dynasty, beating the up-and-coming Dallas Cowboys in weather that was fit only for polar bears. It was two teams, led by two legendary coaches, Vince Lombardi and Tom Landry, refusing to give in to the elements to play a game that revealed the inner character of everyone involved.

I still remember how difficult the loss was for us because we had battled so hard to get back into the game, and when I threw that 50-yard halfback option touchdown pass to Lance Rentzel on the first play of the fourth quarter, we thought this might be our day.

It wasn't, of course, and I remember standing on the sidelines watching the Packers drive down an icy field in awful circumstances to score the game-winning touchdown and realizing that's how champions respond. We outplayed the Packers for most of the game, but when they needed to summon something special, they found a way to do it.

I never forgot that and neither did my teammates. We used that loss as a lesson on how to become champions and we got better. Three years later, we were in our first Super Bowl. The next year, the Cowboys won their first world title.

I'm asked about the Ice Bowl all the time and I never get tired of it because I know it remains a subject many people still want to understand.

And this book celebrates the fiftieth anniversary of that game. It's fun to recall how both teams got to the point of playing at a frozen Lambeau Field and the little dramas that played out before, during, and after the game.

Nobody knew this would be the last game Vince Lombardi would coach before the home crowd. No one knew how much physical, and emotional, damage the game took on those who played and on those who were on hand to watch. And no one knew then that this game would still be talked about today.

So enjoy the journey down this cold, icy memory lane. It's a trip never to be forgotten.

Dan Reeves
June 2017

Dan Reeves played eight seasons for the Cowboys from 1965 to 1972, and served as an assistant coach with them from 1974 to 1980. He had a twenty-three-year head coaching career with the Denver Broncos, New York Giants, and Atlanta Falcons from 1981 to 2003.

INTRODUCTION

THE MEMORIES REMAIN. So do the scars. And both run deep and have lasted for decades.

"I'll never forget that game," said Bob Lilly.

"It was an honor to be a part of it," said Chuck Mercein.

Bob Lilly, a defensive tackle for the Dallas Cowboys, is in the Pro Football Hall of Fame, one of the best to ever play his position in the history of the game. Yet he still sees that final, dramatic play, frozen in time in more ways than one, and helpless to change the result of a game that was in doubt until the end.

Chuck Mercein is not in the Hall of Fame, but he's still famous. A journeyman fullback pressed into service for the Green Bay Packers because the starter was injured, he made the most of a few plays late in the game when his team needed him most and, as a result, he has his place in NFL history, too.

Bob Lilly and Chuck Mercein are two of dozens of performers in a drama that in many ways is still being played out all these years later.

It is known as the Ice Bowl and even the most casual football fan knows about it fifty years later. They know about the weather and the team and the players and the coaches and the fans who braved the nearly unbearable conditions. They know who won and how it happened and what resulted from it.

And they know that it was a game like no other ever before played in the NFL and, very likely, none since.

It was one of a kind and for those who took part in it, those memories endure and the scars, both physically and emotionally, remain.

Played January 31, 1967, more than 50,000 people filled Green Bay's Lambeau Field to watch amazing players on both teams who looked into the stands and were shocked anyone would brave those conditions to watch a football game.

But what a game it was, pitting the established dynasty of the Green Bay Packers against the up-and-coming powerhouse of the Dallas Cowboys.

The year before, the Packers had beaten the Cowboys in Dallas to win the National Football League championship and then two weeks later, the Packers overwhelmed the Kansas City Chiefs in the first Super Bowl.

But in 1967, the Packers were old and injured and stumbling. Their already legendary head coach, Vince Lombardi, had already decided that when this season ended, his ninth in Green Bay, it would be his last. He was tired and ready for a change and he knew as well as anyone that his run with these Packers players was coming to an end.

His teams had already won four NFL titles (1961, 1962, 1965, and 1966) under his autocratic rule and a fifth was within sight. But the fifty-four-year-old coach knew a fifth would be the toughest, but most important, to attain.

He had drummed into his veteran squad during training camp that no NFL team had won three titles in a row, and that accomplishment would put them in a place no one else had ever been. It was the closest thing to immortality a sports team could have, and Lombardi wanted everyone to know it.

But Lombardi also saw the Cowboys as their greatest challenge. Tom Landry, a friend of his from their coaching days with the New York Giants, was the Cowboys' coach, and Landry was building his team in very much the same way the Packers had built theirs under Lombardi.

In 1966, only their seventh season as an NFL franchise, the Cowboys had pushed the Packers to the limit. In 1967, the Cowboys were a year more mature, but the Packers were a year older—and that was a big difference.

So when the two teams met for the second straight season for the NFL championship, this time in Green Bay, the NFL's future was looking upon its rapidly fading present.

That would have been a dramatic enough backdrop for a sport that was growing exponentially in popularity.

What put this game into the annals of NFL lore was the fact that it kicked off in a minus 45 degree wind chill that dropped to minus 65 by the end of the game. The field, already frozen when the game began due to malfunctioning heating coils under the turf, was a sheet of ice by the time it was over.

NFL commissioner Pete Rozelle briefly considered postponing the game but understood the drama that could play out in this little corner of Wisconsin. It was the kings of the NFL against the upstart contenders playing in the kind of weather that would reward survival more than the final score.

And in the end, the game was everything it was meant to be and more. A great start by the Packers was followed by a comeback from the Cowboys that put them the lead. And on the final desperate drive, the tired, battered Packers found enough to drive the length of the field, with help from the previously unknown Mercein, to score the winning touchdown in the final seconds.

But there was so much to it than that.

In the locker room afterward, grown men wept at not having won or lost, but having survived what many said was the toughest experience they ever had on a football field.

The Packers' unflappable quarterback, Bart Starr, who had scored the winning touchdown, was so overwhelmed with what had been accomplished that he had to be reminded they still had another game to play—Super Bowl II two weeks later against the AFL champion Oakland Raiders.

In the aftermath of what came to be know forever and always as Ice Bowl, several players suffered from frostbite and lung damage from the cold weather. Even today, players from both teams talk about what it was like to be part of the game and how it left an impact on them all these years later.

But more than that, they know they took part in a game that was truly something special. It was a game that pitted two of the great NFL franchises against each other and featured fourteen eventual Hall of Famers, including both head coaches.

It was also a game that perhaps did more than any other to show a still dubious American sports audience that pro football was the sport of the future.

It has now been fifty years since the Ice Bowl was played and it continues to resonate. These days, cold weather NFL games are always measured against that one and usually found wanting. There may have been games played in colder weather (though not many) but none has approached the drama, significance, and impact of that one.

The joke among Green Bay Packers fans is that nearly every one claims that either they were at the game or, if they weren't, some family member certainly was. "I just met the 500,000th fan who attended the Ice Bowl," Mercein joked recently.

Even today Mercein, a Yale graduate who went on to a successful career on Wall Street, says a week doesn't go by that he isn't asked about the game.

Former Cowboys linebacker Lee Roy Jordan says his hands still ache in cool weather that he insists were damaged in that game. What hurts him even more in the reality that more people ask him about the Ice Bowl than the Cowboys' Super Bowl VI win or, for that matter, anything else from his stellar fourteen-year career.

Walt Garrison, a second-year running back for the Cowboys that season and who developed a reputation over his nine-year career as one of the toughest players in the game, couldn't believe fans actually showed up to watch.

"I was sitting on the bench with [fullback] Don Perkins and I turned to him and said, 'Can you believe the people who showed up for this,'" he said with a laugh. "I said, 'I'm only here because I was getting paid.' It was pretty incredible."

Cowboys wide receiver Bob Hayes, the 1964 Olympic gold medalist in the 100 meters who by extension was given the title "The World's Fastest Man," was so impacted by the weather that he spent nearly the entire game with his hands shoved down his pants. It became so obvious that the Packers defense knew every time there was a running play because Hayes would keep his hands in pants, taking him out of the game plan. Afterward, he swore he'd never set foot in Green Bay again.

"I remember the defensive linemen told me they weren't going to wear gloves because they wouldn't be able to use their hands to make any tackles," Lee Roy Jordan said. "So I decided I wasn't going to wear them either. After the first series I said, 'To hell with this, I'm wearing gloves.'"

There are a thousand stories from every corner of Lambeau Field that day. Stories of courage and survival brought about for no other reason than the players on the field had no other choice. It was time to play and you played, no matter the conditions.

And for football fans everywhere, this remains their game. It has been replayed on TV over and over again and players have been interviewed and majestic stories have been written about the courage and fortitude of those who took part.

That tells some of the story but, perhaps, not all of it. Maybe the whole story may never be known, and maybe that's as it should be. There will be parts of the Ice Bowl that will remain tucked away in the memory of those who were there and experienced it.

In 2017, a football game played fifty years ago is still remembered, still celebrated, still analyzed, and still remains the seminal moment in the lives of those players who took part. It has taken its place among the top sporting events played in American history, and it is a lengthy, impressive list that spans the decades.

It has been fifty years since Starr snuck into the end zone for the game-winning touchdown that moved the Packers, the NFL, and American sports forward. But in more ways than we can count, our memories tell us it was played just yesterday.

And it always will be.

1

THE LEGEND

THE YEAR 1967 was staggering to a close. On December 31, when the Green Bay Packers and the Dallas Cowboys played a football game to decide the championship of the National Football League, most Americans had had enough of the 364 days that had come before.

It was a year of tragedy that had included the death of three US astronauts who had died in a horrific fire while training for the first Apollo mission, the program that was supposed to put Americans on the moon.

It was a year of conflict as more US soldiers were sent to Vietnam to combat an enemy few in this country understood.

It was a year of protest as anti-war demonstrations, angry and growing, sprung up across the country, from New York City to Madison, Wisconsin, to San Francisco and elsewhere.

It was a year of tension as the war turned many college campuses into smoldering cauldrons and racial divides brought major cities to the brink of anarchy.

It was a year of uncertainty as Americans looked inward to find answers and were puzzled when none could be found.

Even the president, Lyndon Johnson, was losing faith in himself and in a government that he believed could always be counted on to solve America's problems.

Of course, it was also the year that the Beatles unveiled *Sgt. Pepper's Lonely Hearts Club Band*, considered by many the greatest rock album ever created.

It was the Summer of Love when thousands of kids around the country celebrated everything that needed to be celebrated.

It was the year when Thurgood Marshall was confirmed as the first African American Supreme Court Justice.

It had been a long, tough, turbulent year that was made even more poignant by the fact that the year to follow would only be worse.

But that was another problem for another time.

Still, as uncertainty and tension roiled the country, there was the escape of sports.

In 1967, the St. Louis Cardinals beat the Boston Red Sox to win the World Series. The Philadelphia 76ers, led by Wilt Chamberlain, lost only thirteen games in the regular season, then eliminated the powerful Boston Celtics before winning the NBA title. Flashy, mercurial Muhammad Ali claimed the heavyweight boxing title but, in a reflection of an America that was changing rapidly, was suspended because of his refusal to register for the military draft.

And in January of that year, the Green Bay Packers had solidified their place as pro football's dominant franchise by first toying with, and then crushing, the Kansas City Chiefs of the upstart American Football League to win the first-ever Super Bowl in a half-full Los Angeles Coliseum.

The Packers of the 1960s were America's comfort food. Since the fiery Vince Lombardi had stepped in as head coach in 1959, the once pathetic and forgettable franchise located somewhere in the wilds of Wisconsin had become a powerhouse.

Football fans everywhere knew the Packers and how good they were. In time, nine players from those Packers would be elected into the Pro Football Hall of Fame. They were that good and every other player in the league looked at the Packers and how they approached and knew what it take to get to the same level.

They had won four NFL titles (1961, 1962, 1965, and 1966) and they did it not with flash or excitement but with relentless execution and perfection. They didn't do much but what they did, they did superbly, and no one could stop them.

Even the inception of the Super Bowl that year did not slow down the Packers as they beat the best team the rival AFL had to offer. And they barely broke a sweat doing it.

So as 1967 drew to a close, a year that had not gone as anyone really expected, weary Americans saw a familiar and soothing sight—the Packers were again competing for a championship—and, maybe, everything would be OK after all.

"I mean, we were the Packers," said that year's starting center Ken Bowman, an insightful, thoughtful athlete who in the offseason studied to earn his law degree. "We were a dynasty."

But now they had a challenger in the Dallas Cowboys, who had nearly beaten the Packers in the NFL title game the year before. They wanted what the Packers had and they were convinced this was the year.

So on this last day of 1967, Americans were ready to celebrate a new year and a new start and the Packers and Cowboys would close it out with their league championship game. It was just the respite a weary America needed. It was a chance to sit back, take a deep breath, and watch the two best teams in football play for the right to go to the second Super Bowl.

It was a fitting end to a forgettable year.

Or was it?

Professional football was carving its place into the American sports psyche. It had already overtaken the traditionally popular sports of horse racing and boxing and was zeroing in on baseball.

Pro football on television was a feast for the eyes with its violent hits, charismatic players, and subtle intricacies. There were teams in major markets such as Cleveland, Los Angeles, New York, and Chicago but the best team, amazingly, was from a small town in the corner of Wisconsin and fans loved that too.

The league had played its first "world championship" in early January with the Packers rolling over the Chiefs and it had hit a chord.

Now the NFL was ready for the second Super Bowl, a name invented by then-Kansas City Chiefs owner Lamar Hunt after he saw his child playing with that year's latest toy craze, the Super Ball.

It was expected that the NFL, older and more established, would again dominate the game, this time to be played in Miami, Florida.

Indeed, most league officials, media, and fans believed that the real "world championship" would be played two weeks before Super Bowl II when the NFL staged its title game.

So when the Packers beat the Los Angeles Rams, 28–7, at Milwaukee County Stadium and the Cowboys clobbered the Cleveland Browns, 52–14, at the Cotton Bowl in the first round of the playoffs, it set up the second straight meeting between the two teams in the championship.

And all of America wanted to watch that.

"It was at a time when the game was extremely popular," said Cowboys running back Dan Reeves. "And you had two extremely popular teams as well. You had Lombardi and Landry and [Packers quarterback Bart] Starr and [Cowboys quarterback Don] Meredith. It had everything."

The two teams had met the year before in much the same circumstances. The Packers had posted a 12–2 record and won the West Division thanks to the NFL's top defense. The Cowboys won the East with a 10–3–1 record and the league's highest scoring offense.

The two franchises had never faced each other before in the playoffs until that game at the Cotton Bowl. The two teams had been evenly matched and whacked away on each other all day before a Don Meredith interception in the closing seconds at the Packers 1-yard line had sealed a 34–27 Packers victory.

Green Bay had been pushed and pushed by a relatively new team that was playing the game a little differently than they did.

The Packers moved on two weeks later to beat the Chiefs in the Super Bowl while the Cowboys learned from their mistakes and vowed to be back.

And so they were.

On New Year's Eve 1967, the Cowboys traveled to Green Bay, a place Cowboys coach Tom Landry hated playing, to face the Cowboys for the NFL title.

In his weekly TV show a few days before the game, Vince Lombardi smiled wearily.

"I'm glad the game is in Green Bay," he said. "The weather's supposed to beautiful."

2

THE REALITY

NO ONE REALLY knows who first coined the term *Ice Bowl*. More than likely, it was a line in the game story written by one of the army of sportswriters on hand to witness the drama.

It was probably a throwaway line, inserted by one of the writers to try and convey what they had witnessed that afternoon. Was it a clever line? Not especially, but it would become one of those phrases that would endure for generations.

Yet "Ice Bowl" summed up events nicely. It set the tone that the entire stadium, all the fans and players and the entire city of Green Bay were somehow encased in an icy prison from which there was no escape. That meant everyone would remain exactly where they were until a result was reached. And that led to the belief that this was not a football game as much as it was a test of wills.

As a result, it would end up being the perfect line to encapsulate a game that is still being talked about fifty years later.

"I think what still makes it special was probably the conditions as much as anything," Dan Reeves said. "You just don't see that much anymore with so many indoor stadiums and so much equipment to handle the weather. We didn't have that then. I know a lot of games call themselves 'ice bowls' over the years but very few games can come close to those conditions and with what was on the line in that game. There may have been big games played in cold weather but not for a league championship. Not like this."

The legend of the first, last, and only Ice Bowl took shape even before the game began.

Professional football had been played in Green Bay since 1919 when a fellow named Curly Lambeau who was able to get his employer, the Indian Packing Company, to kick in $500 for uniforms and equipment. In return, Lambeau named the team the Packers and two years later they would help form the foundation of the National Football League.

The Packers would go on to be one of the league's first great dynasties, winning championships in 1929, 1930, and 1931 and again in 1935, 1939, and 1944. Along the way, they'd produce the first crop of NFL Hall of Famers including Curly Lambeau, Cal Hubbard, Johnny "Blood" McNally, Don Hutson, Mike Michalske, and Clarke Hinkle.

But professional football was still a novelty in many parts of the country—a violent, dangerous game that was not necessarily appropriate for polite society.

Still, when early football fans thought of the NFL, the Packers were the team many people focused on. In a country that was growing in stature and prominence on the world stage, the Packers represented the traits of everything America wanted to be—dominance, excellence, and quality.

But it didn't last. It never does.

A disgruntled Curly Lambeau left the Packers, and those great players of the early years did what all players do—they got older and retired. And by the late 1940s, the Packers fell into mediocrity. By the 1950s, they had become all but irrelevant and, indeed, if not for infusion of cash, the Packers might well have folded.

But they survived and by 1959, more changes were on the way. Vince Lombardi, the offensive coordinator for the New York Giants, was named Green Bay's coach, replacing the hopelessly overmatched Ray McLean, and for the next nine years, the Packers changed the entire landscape of the NFL.

But if the Packers were the NFL's landed gentry of the league, the Dallas Cowboys were the newcomers, the arrogant kids who felt there was a new way to play the game would show everyone how to do it.

Like the Packers, the Cowboys dipped into the New York Giants staff and took their defensive coordinator, Tom Landry, to be their first head coach.

The Packers had been established in 1919 while the Cowboys were born in 1960, the NFL's first modern franchise team. The Packers had a storied history, and championships and were the past and present of the NFL. The Cowboys? They respected the Packers but saw themselves as the future of the league. And they knew that to become the best, they had to take out the best. And at the time, that was the Packers.

The reality of that situation hit the Cowboys in that inaugural season of 1960. In November, the Cowboys traveled the City Stadium in Green Bay (later to be renamed Lambeau Field) to face a Green Bay team in its second season under Lombardi.

Green Bay, which would go on to play for the NFL championship that year (losing to the Philadelphia Eagles), toyed with the young Cowboys that day, forcing five turnovers and winning, 41–7. It was a template for how the Packers would dominate teams for the next eight years. Fullback Jim Taylor ran for 121 yards and three touchdowns and linebacker Ray Nitschke took an interception back for a touchdown as Dallas was held to 261 total yards.

The Cowboys didn't win a game that season, going 0–11–1, but they learned lessons that would prove valuable to them as the years went by. And they were using the Packers as the team they needed to become if they were going to be successful.

Using Landry's innovative "flex" defense and counting on an offense that played efficiently but without flash, Landry quickly made the Cowboys a force to be reckoned with. The Packers beat the Cowboys in regular season games in both 1964 and 1965, but the margin between the two teams was closing.

Landry and his players saw that. More importantly, so did Lombardi and his players.

In 1966, they would play in a game that truly mattered.

3

THE COACHES

BART STARR ALWAYS enjoyed telling the story about his first encounter with the man who would eventually change the course of his football career, not to mention the course of his life.

In a 1958 preseason game against the New York Giants, Starr, who was then a struggling quarterback for a bad Packers team, recalled the force of nature that was Vince Lombardi.

"We were playing the game in Boston and, like Milwaukee County Stadium, the benches were on the same side of the field,"

Starr recalled years later. "We had scored a touchdown and I was jogging off the field after holding for the extra point and as I was going past the Giants bench, I see this guy ranting and raving at the defensive line players for the Giants."

Starr paused and laughed at the memory.

"To show you his aggressiveness and intensity, he was yelling at the defensive players and he was the offensive coordinator."

That was Vince Lombardi, a roiling sea of emotion and passion and competitiveness who always delivered his message with all the subtlety of a baseball bat to the forehead.

In that meaningless preseason game, it is not known how the coach who ran the Giants defense reacted to Lombardi's fulminating at his charges. It's more than likely, though, that Tom Landry simply shook his head and went back to work, understanding as many already did, that it was just a case of Lombardi being Lombardi.

They made a great team, Landry and Lombardi. They had come together in 1954 when Jim Lee Howell was named the Giants' head coach, replacing Steve Owen.

Of course, neither knew in those days when the NFL was still seeking to establish its reputation that the two of them would collide on a frozen field in Green Bay, Wisconsin, and produce a game that still reverberates today.

Lombardi joined the Giants staff that year after beginning his coaching career at St. Cecilia's High School in New Jersey and then successful stints collegiate coaching stints at his alma mater, Fordham University, and then as offensive line coach for four seasons at Army under the tutelage of legendary head coach Red Blaik.

When the chance came to become an offensive coordinator, Lombardi leaped at it, convinced it was the next step to attaining his ultimate goal—to be an NFL head coach.

Landry was already well established with the Giants by the time Lombardi arrived. He had an impressive background, and not just as a football player. A native of Mission, Texas, he played one season at the University of Texas before he enlisted in the Army Air Force in 1943.

He ended up flying thirty B-17 missions over Europe and had to deal with the death of his brother and a crash landing during the war.

He returned to the University of Texas in 1946 where he played fullback, quarterback, and some defensive back and was part of a Longhorns team that won the 1948 Sugar Bowl and the 1949 Orange Bowl.

He played one professional season for the New York Yankees of the ill-fated All-America Football Conference and then signed with the Giants in 1950.

Even that first season, head coach Steve Owen saw that Landry had the leadership skills to be a terrific coach and by 1954, when Jim Lee Howell took over as head coach, he was the Giants' player-coach, a defensive back who also coached the defense.

He retired as a player after the 1955 season and slid into the defensive coordinator role full-time in 1956.

By then, Lombardi had been the offensive coordinator for two seasons and had established an offense that was hard-nosed, emotional, and talented.

The two coaches could not have been more different, and that's exactly what Howell was seeking.

Landry, tall and languid and as unknowable as the Texas landscape he came from, had already established himself as cerebral
and innovative. Lombardi, a loud, emotional New Yorker, had
built the offense in his profane, raucous image.

Whether Lombardi and Landry were friends in the truest sense
of the word was up for debate.

"I think they were friends," Dan Reeves would say later. "As
much as anything, they had a respect for each other as much as a
friendship."

Frank Gifford, the Giants' talented running back who flourished under Lombardi, told David Maraniss in *When Pride Still
Mattered* that there was always a creative tension between the two
men.

"There was a lot of competition between Lombardi and Landry and I don't know if that ever turned into a friendship," he
said. "That filtered through the team itself. There was a tension
We didn't like [the defense] and they didn't like us much. And
we didn't really care. We were cliquey."

For their parts, Landry and Lombardi insisted there was a
friendship there that, perhaps, no one except the two of them
could understand.

But one thing was certain—everyone in the league knew that
the Giants had the best duo of offensive and defensive coordina-
tors in the league and that, one day soon, both would be head
coaches.

And their competitiveness would last for years.

Each brought specific gifts to their position. Landry, perhaps
based on his industrial engineering background (his major at
Texas), could dissect and analyze situations before anyone else.

His players did not love him (either in New York or Dallas) because he was too remote for that. But they played hard for him because they knew he was usually the smartest guy in the room.

Lombardi was the exact opposite. Whereas Landry dismissed emotion as part of the game, Lombardi demanded it. Passion and aggressiveness was the key to being successful. He formulated that in New York and perfected it in Green Bay.

Wellington Mara, the owner of the Giants at the time, was asked about the two highly regarded assistant coaches.

Both were special, he said, but Landry had something extra.

"Vince was a pure teacher, but he could not get what he wanted off films as quick as Tom," he once said. "In fact, there were few people who were as quick a study as Tom."

So with Landry running the defense and Lombardi in charge of the offense, the Giants became an NFL powerhouse of the late 1950s. In fact, in the five seasons Lombardi and Landry were together in New York, the Giants did not have a losing season. Unfortunately, for two driven men like those two, they only managed one championship as well.

That came in 1956 when the Giants obliterated the Chicago Bears, 47–7, behind the running of Gifford and Alex Webster and precision passing of Charlie Conerly and Landry's defense that held the Bears to 270 total yards and forced three turnovers.

The Giants returned to the championship game two years later against the Baltimore Colts in the game that would come to be known in many circles as "the greatest game ever played."

Maybe it was or maybe another game, set to be played nine years later, involving two of the same coaches, might vie for that title.

This much is certain about the 1958 NFL Championship played at windy, wild Yankee Stadium: That game, won by the Colts in the first overtime in league championship history, set the NFL on its course to becoming the country's most popular sport.

It was a game that saw Landry and Lombardi at their best and, in some ways, at their worst. Their genius and their flaws were both on display, and both men learned valuable lessons as the years went by.

The Colts, led by their remarkable quarterback Johnny Unitas, graceful wide receiver Raymond Berry, and thunderous fullback Alan Ameche, tore up Landry's proud defense. Meanwhile, Lombardi's offense, stymied for much of the first half, finally came to life only to fizzle again at the worst possible time.

As Giants fans can recount even now, the game seemed in control as they had rallied to take a 17–14 lead. With a little more than two minutes to play and facing third down and three yards to go from the New York 43, Frank Gifford ran for what seemed like a first down that would put the game out of reach and give the Giants their second title in three years.

But the officials marked the ball short of the first down marker and both Howell and Lombardi decided instead of taking a gamble on fourth down, to punt back to the Colts and let Landry's terrific defense close it out.

Instead, Unitas marched the Colts downfield, frustrating New York by throwing primarily short passes to Berry, until they reached the Giants 13-yard line where Steve Myhra kicked a 20-yard field goal on the final play to tie the game at 17–17.

Heading into the overtime, a relatively new concept where the first team to score would win, Landry knew his defense was on its heels and exhausted. The Giants actually won the coin toss and got the ball first. Once again, facing a 4th-and-1 situation just as he had at the end of regulation, Howell made the decision to punt. It was not a decision Lombardi disagreed with. This time, he thought the defense would make a difference.

But it couldn't. Unitas, sensing a Giants defense that was at its limit, moved the Colts methodically downfield and, after a thirteen-play drive, Ameche smashed into the end zone for the championship-clinching touchdown.

Landry did what he could. He was already a burgeoning defensive genius, but he was no miracle worker. Lombardi could only watch, impotent and furious that his offense could not come through when it needed to.

In truth, Baltimore dominated the game, rolling up 452 total yards on Landry's proud defenders. Unitas had a game that would start him on his path to the Pro Football Hall of Fame, completing 26 of 40 passes for 349 yards. And his last two drives were things of beauty.

Lombardi's offense had its moments but, after a quarterback switch from the struggling Don Heinrich to the wily veteran Conerly, never did find its stride. And Gifford, the star running back, was practically inconsolable afterward. After all, he'd fumbled twice and came up short (apparently) on that third down run at the end of regulation.

But Lombardi found him after the game, hugged him, and said simply, "Frank, we wouldn't have even gotten here without you."

For Lombardi, that agonizing loss felt like the end of the road. He'd spent five years as the Giants' offensive coordinator and built what he considered a solid reputation.

He was ready to be an NFL head coach, and he knew it. But he was also haunted by the memory that he'd already had the opportunity to move up to the head coaching ranks and turned it down.

The year before, the Philadelphia Eagles were in search of a new coach and set their sights on Lombardi. They saw in him a young, hungry, bright coach who had the potential to be great.

But the Eagles were a mess. Since winning back-to-back NFL titles in 1948 and 1949, they had done very little since. Indeed, there had been no playoff appearances and a succession of coaches had been unable to coax anything from the team.

Jim Trimble was fired after four seasons and Hugh Devore had coached the 1956–57 seasons, managing to win just seven games.

On top of the lack of success on the field, the Eagles front office was plagued with bickering, paranoia, and jealousies.

It might be a good situation for some coach, but not Lombardi. At least that's what the Mara family told him. They obviously did not want to lose their prized assistant coach, and especially not to a close rival.

Lombardi was so anxious to be a head coach and feared another opportunity might not make itself available that he initially agreed to coach the Eagles starting in 1958. But the Mara family continued to chirp in his ear about the problems in Philly. They gave him a raise, they offered him more responsibility, and they told him his chance to be a head coach would come soon. Meanwhile, the Eagles kept sweetening the deal.

In *Where Pride Still Mattered*, David Maraniss wrote that Lombardi's wife and confidant, Marie, told her confused husband to go to their local church in Red Bank, New Jersey, sit in a pew and contemplate the future.

"Don't pray," she said. "Think!"

That did the trick. Lombardi turned down the Eagles offer. Philadelphia went on to hire Buck Shaw, the one-time head coach of the San Francisco 49ers who was now coaching at the Air Force Academy. Shaw's first season was awful as the Eagles struggled to a 2–9–1 record. The next season they improved to 7–5 and by 1960, behind the league MVP quarterback Norm Van Brocklin (a major reason Lombardi was intrigued by the Eagles job in the first place) they finished 10–2. They capped that season by winning the NFL championship, beating the Green Bay Packers, 17–13, in Vince Lombardi's second season as Green Bay's head coach.

Now the crushing overtime loss to the Colts in 1958 was the sign Lombardi was waiting for. It was time to move on. And the opportunity that awaited him was in Green Bay.

But if the Eagles in 1957 had been a mess, the Packers in 1959 were a mess times ten. The once-proud franchise had fallen so far that there was serious questions over the years of its viability in the NFL. Worse, it had become all but irrelevant in a league dominated by teams in larger cities.

Since its last league title in 1944, the Packers had managed just three winning seasons. It had driven away its iconic founder, star player and coach Curly Lambeau, and now Green Bay, even in the 1950s, had become the place coaches from other teams would threaten to send any players who weren't performing well.

As bad as it had been for years, rock bottom was finally reached in 1958 when the Packers posted a 1–10–1 record, the worst in franchise history. The head coach, Ray "Scooter" McLean was an amiable fellow whom the players genuinely liked—which may have been part of the problem.

McLean lasted just that one season before he was let go, a decision that left many in the front office in tears because he was such a nice guy.

Now the Packers focused their attention on Lombardi, the fire-breather from the Giants who might be able to mold a roster that already had genuinely talent.

In fact, the Packers roster of 1958 that won a single game included offensive linemen Forrest Gregg and Jerry Kramer; half-back Paul Hornung; fullback Jim Taylor; quarterback Bart Starr; and wide receiver Max McGee. There was also future Hall of Famers Jim Ringo and Len Ford, star linebacker Dan Currie, and defensive back Jess Whittenton.

Lombardi saw the talent there and knew, with the right plan and the right way to teach, this team could be something special. And that opportunity intrigued him.

But, once again, Wellington Mara was reluctant to see Lombardi leave, and he wasn't sure the Packers' situation was any better than that of the Eagles.

Nonetheless, he gave the Packers permission to interview Lombardi though, ironically enough, he suggested that Packers team president Dominic Olejniczak might want to talk his other top assistant first. Maybe Tom Landry, he suggested, would be a better fit? But Olejniczak, under pressure from the Packers board of directors to find the right fit for a team that desperately needed it, wanted to talk with Lombardi first.

But other events were swirling at the time. Lombardi knew the head coaching job at West Point would be opening up. Red Blaik, Lombardi's mentor, was retiring and Lombardi had long seen himself settling in at the military academy, coaching a steady stream of players who had the type of discipline that he demanded.

It could be an interesting and challenging move for him. But Lombardi soon learned that he would not be a candidate as West Point decided to stick with its long established tradition of hiring a coach who had gone through the academy.

Lombardi swallowed hard at that explanation and, while disappointed, he set his sights on the Green Bay job though, as it turned out, he was no lock for that either.

Jim Trimble, who ironically had been one of the head coaches with the Eagles who had not survived and had led to Lombardi being considered for the Philadelphia job in 1958, was a strong candidate. He had spent the previous two seasons coaching the Hamilton Tiger-Cats of the Canadian Football League and was anxious to return to the NFL. But Trimble turned out not to be a serious candidate after all.

Another candidate, and probably the frontrunner in the minds of many observers, was Forest Evashevski, the successful head coach at the University of Iowa. In late January of 1959, Evashevski and the Packers met secretly in Green Bay to discuss the position, but the Iowa coach left after a few hours after realizing it was not what he was seeking.

That moved Lombardi back to the top of Green Bay's list and, from there, the Packers moved quickly.

Mara again gave the Packers permission to interview Lombardi for the head coaching position but with the stipulation that if the Giants' head coaching came open, he could be released to discuss it.

The Packers' offer was impressive. Not only would Lombardi be the head coach, a job he had coveted for years, he would be the general manager, the guy in charge of bringing in the talent that he would coach. He would be the man, as another successful New York head coach Bill Parcells would say decades later, the person who would purchase the groceries and cook the meal. It was too much to turn down.

Even so, after agreeing to take the position, Lombardi was suddenly riddled with uncertainty. Green Bay? Really? His headstrong and closest advisor, his wife Marie, had more than a few doubts. She loved New York and the thought of moving to Wisconsin (Wisconsin?) was more than she could imagine. She even pleaded with Wellington Mara to talk to her husband and convince him to turn it down, just as he had done the year before with the Eagles position.

But this time was different and even the Giants' powerful owner could see that. And he told Marie that unlike Philadelphia, Green Bay was the place for him.

When word of Lombardi's hiring was made public, the reaction among Packers fans was a confused shrug.

A New York guy who had never been a head coach before. Sure, he'd been a great assistant coach but being a head coach in Green Bay was a different animal. There had not been a great Packers head coach since the Curly Lambeau era ended ten years earlier and no one was expecting miracles from this new guy.

However, George Halas, already a legend as the founder and head coach of the rival Chicago Bears, reportedly was furious at Olejniczak for hiring Lombardi because he knew that under his tutelage, the Packers would once again be competitive.

One Packer was also anxious to see what the new guy to do. Bart Starr, the Packers seventeenth-round draft in 1956 and who was beginning to have doubts if he belonged in the league, recalled to the very word his first meeting with the new coach.

"He looked us in the eye and said, 'Gentlemen we are always going to relentlessly chase perfection, knowing full well we will not catch it because nothing is perfect. In the process, we will catch excellence.' Then he paused and said, 'I'm not remotely interested in being just good.' We all knew immediately there would be a change. I called my wife back in Alabama and said, 'Honey, we're going to begin to win.' It was an absolutely wonderful experience."

Another player who felt, or at least hoped, a change was in the air was running back Paul Hornung. The 1956 Heisman Trophy winner from Notre Dame had been the Packers' top draft pick in 1957 and had grown increasingly more frustrated in his two years in Green Bay.

Neither his first coach, Lisle Blackbourn nor his second, Scooter McLean, had known what to do with the versatile player. Was he a running back? A quarterback? A wide receiver? A defensive back? All of the above? None of the above?

All Hornung knew was that he was not getting a chance to showcase his skills and after the disastrous 1958 season, he was seriously thinking of retiring and pursuing a career as an actor.

Then, three months after being hired as head coach, Lombardi sent a letter to Hornung, leaving no doubt the plans he had for the player.

In part the letter read, *"I would like you to report to Green Bay on Monday, July 13, 1959. With the installation of a new system for the Packers, it is imperative that we get off to a good start and I expect you to report in top physical condition. We will start running immediately and I suggest you report to training camp at a maximum of 207 pounds. You will be heavy enough at that weight and left halfback in my system must have speed in order capitalize on the running pass option play."*

There it was. In just a few short lines, Lombardi had clearly stated that Hornung would be the featured back in an offense that would emphasize the run. It's exactly what Hornung was looking for and, in the seasons to follow, he would not only flourish in Lombardi's system but become, perhaps, Lombardi's favorite player. And it would culminate with Hornung's 1986 induction into the Pro Football Hall of Fame.

"He was exactly what we needed," Hornung would say of Lombardi.

Tom Landry's journey to the Dallas Cowboys as their head coach was something far less dramatic. Unlike the single-mindedness of Lombardi who needed to get to the top of the coaching pyramid as quickly as possible to prove himself, Landry's approach was more analytical, which, of course, was how Landry approached nearly everything in his life.

Perhaps his view was forged during World War II when he flew B-17 bomber missions in Europe. After all, he had seen things during that war that he would never forget and made him realize that to overreact to situations might be the difference between life and death.

In truth, Landry had given very little thought to being a head coach until the time when his name was everywhere. He had formed the dynamic duo with Lombardi and for several years those two were linked, perhaps reluctantly, as the best offensive and defensive assistant coaches in the NFL.

Lombardi had been the first to take the plunge, agreeing in 1959 to become head coach and general manager of a Green Bay Packers franchise that was seeking to find itself after years in the wilderness.

Landry remained with the Giants in 1959, perfecting what was at first the novel 4-3 defense (four down linemen and three linebackers) which was now being adopted by other NFL teams.

He still loved the intricacies that creating a defense could provide. He had a way of looking at a rival offense, finding its weaknesses and then developing a way to attack it. To him, great defense was every bit as exciting as a great run or a long touchdown pass. His job was to make sure he had his players in the right place and when they were, there was nothing more beautiful.

It was that overall attitude and approach that would lead him to develop the innovative umbrella-like "flex" defense in Dallas that dominated the NFL for years.

Landry's defense continued to be one of the NFL's best that season, allowing a league-low 170 points, as the Giants posted a 10–2 record. One of the wins that season came over Lombardi's new team, which was still learning his way to play.

The Giants held the Packers to 160 total yards as the Giants cruised to an easy 20–3 win. The Packers were in the midst of a five-game losing streak when they played the Giants but soon righted themselves and finished the season 7–5, the team's first winning season since 1947 and the first glimpse of hope in years for their fans.

The Giants reached the NFL championship game for the second straight year, again facing the Colts. But unlike the heartbreak of the year before when the New York defense collapsed and lost in overtime, the Colts defense forced three turnovers and beat the Giants, 31–16.

Johnny Unitas, the Colts' quarterback who had dismantled the Giants the year before, did it again, throwing for 264 yards and two touchdowns and rallying the Colts to their second straight title even the Giants' defense allowed only 280 total yards.

But even Landry, who had spent the past ten years with the Giants as a player, player/coach and then defensive coordinator, knew it was time to try something else.

Pro football was changing dramatically, and Landry found himself in the forefront. In an effort to provide competition for the more established NFL as well as to meet the exploding interest in pro football, the American Football League was formed.

AFL owners wanted to exploit the growing population centers in the south and west and made a point of placing two teams in Texas—Houston and Dallas.

As a native Texan and as perhaps the hottest head-coaching prospect around, Landry was wooed hard by the two Texas teams, especially Houston.

But the NFL saw what was happening and quickly established a franchise of its own in Dallas that would, after several fits and starts, become known as the Cowboys. The team owner, Texas millionaire Clint Murchison, desperately wanted Landry as his head coach.

But in a situation not unlike what Lombardi faced in 1959, Giants' owner Wellington Mara tried to hang on to Landry.

Current Giants coach Jim Lee Howell was likely to step aside after the 1960 season and Landry would be next in line, he was told.

But the chance to return to Texas and get in on the ground floor with a brand new franchise was appealing to Landry. So when Cowboys team president Tex Schramm offered Landry the job, he took it, telling his wife Alicia, "Oh well, we might as well try it. We'll probably get fired in two or three years but what the heck."

Indeed, had football not worked out for Landry, he was perfectly content to walk away and use his engineering degree and go into the oil business.

But football did work out for Landry and with his combination of football acumen and his unusual tendency to remain above emotional outbursts, unheard of in a sport where emotion is such a part of the game's fabric, made him unique.

Some who watched thought him a bloodless autocrat whose interest in his players stopped and started on the playing field. And in some ways, that was true. Landry could not afford the wasted energy of emotional explosions when there was so much teaching that needed to be done.

In some ways, he had envied Lombardi's ability to erupt one minute and then put his arm around a player and tell him how important he was the next. That wasn't Landry and he knew it long before he took over as a head coach. He was a teacher and he wanted to be the best one he could be.

And those who knew him, those who played for him, knew how precisely he focused on football and how there was a reason for everything he did.

Giants team owner Wellington Mara once called Landry "the quietest cocky man I ever met," a distinction Landry did not argue with.

By 1960, both Landry and Lombardi had moved on to their respective new assignments. Lombardi was in his second season as Green Bay's head coach and, already, there was a different feeling. He had installed his run first offense and began getting the people in place to make it work.

Already, Lombardi had installed and was perfecting the "Packers Sweep" that would haunt defenses around the NFL for years to come. And in Dallas, despite the million and one details needed to make his new team competitive, Landry was paying attention to what his old friend was up to.

He saw that in Lombardi's offense, which was coined "run to daylight," there were eight gaps along the line of scrimmage, six between offensive linemen, and two on the edges, or the flats. In response, Landry assigned a defender to plug each gap. The idea was for each defender to keep his "gap" discipline and wait for a ball carrier to show up where he was. It was wasted motion for a defender to seek out the ballcarrier while leaving another unguarded.

Landry had been down this road before while playing and coaching with the Giants. In 1950, he had created an "umbrella" defense to slow down the passing game of the powerful Cleveland Browns. In 1958, to counter the challenges presented by the best running back of the generation, Cleveland's Jim Brown, Landry implemented the 4-3 defense that placed the emphasis on covering gaps.

In Landry's view, the defense would be the hallmark of his teams and not simply because defense is what he knew best. His plan was to teach his defenders to anticipate, to recognize, and to react to everything they saw, making it difficult for opposing offenses to move the ball.

It was a great plan and, in time, it figured to be a success. But that was the key phrase: in time. The Cowboys did not have the personnel yet to make its plans flourish but, given time, it would.

Not surprisingly, the Cowboys struggled in their early years, but the pieces were already starting to come together.

One player who saw what Landry was doing and embraced it was linebacker Lee Roy Jordan, who was drafted in 1963.

"He was a great coach and a great leader and great evaluator of talent," Jordan said. "He brought that team in and grew it in a tremendous fashion. We made so much progress in the early sixties."

Jordan was among the early converts to Landry's belief that to shut down an opposing it was necessary to shut down the run first.

"His statement was, 'If we control the run we'll make them pass. Then we'll control the passing routes," Jordan said. "He convinced us all that it would work. And a lot of it did because we led the league in defense for a few seasons. He gave us the keys to get the places we needed to be. He had it all worked out."

In his head, perhaps, but on the field it would take a while.

In 1960, the new Cowboys staggered to 0–11–1 inaugural season, but Don Meredith, a tough and smart Texas kid from Southern Methodist, was already in place as quarterback.

In 1961, they would post a 4–9–1 record while adding more pieces to the puzzle including running back Don Perkins, defensive back Warren Livingston, linebacker Chuck Howley, and eventual Hall of Fame defensive tackle Bob Lilly.

The Cowboys suffered through another losing season in 1962 (5–8–1), but more pieces were added to the puzzle including defensive end George Andrie, defensive backs Mike Gaechter and Cornell Green, and tight end Pettis Norman.

In 1963, linebacker Lee Roy Jordan and offensive lineman Tony Liscio were added as the Cowboys sputtered to a 4–10 season and in 1964, Dallas went to 5–8–1 but saw key additions to the roster include offensive linemen Jim Boeke and Dave Manders, linebacker Dave Edwards, and defensive back Mel Renfro.

By the 1965 season, when wide receiver Bob Hayes, offensive lineman Ralph Neely, defensive tackle Jethro Pugh, and running back Dan Reeves joined the team, the Cowboys were in a position to contend.

"We felt like we were building something pretty special," Jordan said. "We were adding players every year that were substantial. We started out with Bob Lilly and then we got linebackers like Chuck Howley and Dave Edwards and then I came along and I helped solidify the rest of the linebacking corps. Then we added defensive backs like Mel Renfro that were just outstanding players. And we all bought into the defensive concept. We could see what he was doing."

In a *Texas Monthly* magazine story from 1973 that tried to deconstruct the enigma that Landry was already known to be, former Giants defensive back Emlen Tunnell tried, but failed, to put him into perspective.

"Landry was a born student of the game," said Tunnell, who played with Landry as a Giants defensive back and then was coached by him when Landry took over defensive coordinator duties. "But he was kind of weird. After a game, the rest of us would go out for a beer, Tom would disappear. He was always with his family. You never knew what was going on in his mind. He never said nothing, but you always knew what was going on."

And that's exactly the way Landry wanted it.

"Most of us just played the game," Giants running back Frank Gifford once said. "Landry studied it. He was cool and calculating. Emotion had no place in his makeup."

That's exactly the way he wanted that, too.

After all, Landry not only had the sobering experience of World War II that would burn itself into his brain for the rest of his life, he was also a first-rate industrial engineering student in college who would have gone into that field had football not suited him so well.

He analyzed everything to the point that his players often tuned him out. But they also knew that if they went where he told them to go, chances were they'd succeed.

As for his lack of emotion, that was all part of the plan, too.

He once said, "The reason I take on the appearance of being unemotional is I don't believe you can be emotional and concentrate the way you must to be effective. When I see a great play on the sideline, I can't cheer it. I'm a couple plays ahead, thinking."

It was the perfect paradox between Landry and his rival Lombardi.

Packers players feared making a mistake and having Lombardi yell at them because he would question their manhood. Cowboys players feared making a mistake because Landry would look at them coolly. His nickname was, after all, "Plastic Man." They were meant to feel like something less than human. Packers players were meant to feel all-too-human.

Yet somehow, both coaches found themselves in the ideal positions to wield control the only way they knew how.

But even as his Cowboys struggled in their early years and there were calls for Landry to change, he stubbornly refused. This was the way to win on a long term basis and if he was left alone to do that job, he would get it done.

Indeed, at the end of the 1965 season, when the Cowboys finished with their best record to date at 7-7, Meredith was asked about the future of the Cowboys. His response was more than a little prophetic.

"Landry knows just what kind of personnel he wants at each position, and he knows precisely what he wants to do with them," he said. "When he gets it, the Cowboys and the Packers will be playing for the championship."

The next season, Meredith's words would prove eerily true, first in Dallas after the 1966, and a year later on a frozen field in Green Bay, Wisconsin.

By most accounts, when Lombardi ran off the field after the Ice Bowl, he already knew that would be his final trip up the Lambeau Field walkway as Green Bay's head coach. He knew it was time to give it up even if he still wasn't quite ready to reconcile it just yet.

Though only fifty-four years old at the time, he was already known, usually affectionately, by his players as the "Old Man" and, in truth, even in an era when everyone looked older than they were, Lombardi looked every bit an old man.

The game to which he had given everything, in turn, had taken everything from him. From his days growing up and playing the game in New Jersey to Fordham University to coaching in high school and at West Point and then as one of the NFL's top assistant coaches with the Giants, Lombardi had thrown everything he had into it.

He knew only two speeds to do his job the way it needed to be done: with emotion and with more emotion.

Few escaped his piercing glares and spontaneous bursts of rage.

Hall of Fame defensive tackle Henry Jordan famously said, "Lombardi treated us all the same way—like dogs."

Guard Jerry Kramer, who has perhaps kept the Lombardi legacy alive longer and stronger than anyone, has always been convinced Lombardi changed his life and the lives of many of the players on those teams.

He recalled a time during training camp in 1959 when Lombardi was in his first season as coach and Kramer in his second year as a player.

"I'd had a terrible practice and on the field Lombardi just gave me hell," Kramer said. "He said I couldn't play at this level and why didn't I just quit. So I'm sitting at my locker room and I really am thinking about quitting. He comes up to me and puts his hand behind my neck and says, 'Jerry, you're going to be the best guard in football one day.' I couldn't believe it. That's all I needed to hear. He always had this way of saying the right thing when you needed it most."

In time, of course, Kramer did become one of the best guards in NFL history and he still revels in that memory of Lombardi looking at the replay of Starr's sneak into end zone in the Packers exhausted, jubilant locker room. His eyes bright, Lombardi watched the sequence and Kramer's block that opened the hole and he yelled, "Way to go, Jerry!"

"That meant everything to me," Kramer said.

Not every player understood the blind devotion and all-encompassing fear that the coach engendered in so many.

Center Ken Bowman, a free-thinking iconoclast who was drafted in 1964, remembers walking down the sidewalk during training camp his rookie season. He was eating an ice cream cone with a veteran player when they saw Lombardi approaching. Immediately, the veteran threw his cone into the bushes so Lombardi wouldn't see it. Bowman kept eating his.

"Lombardi walked by and said 'Hi fellas,' and kept walking," Bowman recalled with a laugh. "That was the impact Lombardi had."

The stories and rumors trailed Lombardi wherever he went.

As general manager, he also negotiated contracts and, in those days, very few players had agents. Players made their own deals.

Jim Taylor, the Packers' leading rusher for many years and a mainstay on the offense, wanted a new deal and remembers how difficult it was getting Lombardi to budge.

"He was very tough to deal with," he said. "You had to negotiate your deal and then win your position. It wasn't easy."

It eventually led to Taylor asking the Packers to make him available for the 1967 expansion draft that would help populate the newly created New Orleans Saints franchise. Louisiana was still home for Taylor and he knew he would not win a looming contract battle with Lombardi.

The most famous, and since debunked story, of Lombardi's infamous negotiating skills involved Hall of Fame center Jim Ringo in 1964. Ringo had toiled for the Packers since 1953, playing for bad teams under four different coaches before Lombardi's arrival.

His career flourished and he was part of Green Bay's first two NFL titles and in as the '64 season loomed, he talked to Lombardi about a raise.

The story, which took on mythic proportions over the years, went that after Ringo demanded a raise, Lombardi excused himself and went into another room. He came out five minutes later and said, "Jim, you've just been traded to the Philadelphia Eagles. Congratulations."

It was a great story and one Lombardi himself perpetuated because he saw agents becoming more and more involved in negotiations and he wasn't happy about it. In truth, Ringo had an agent who did demand a raise for his client. But Ringo wanted a trade, preferably to the Eagles since Philadelphia was home for him.

As well, Lombardi was in the market for a new center as well as a running back and a linebacker and he thought Ringo's best days were behind him. He needed draft picks and this was a way to get it done. He drafted Bowman that year out of Wisconsin.

But Lombardi loved having that story make the rounds of the league. Though almost entirely untrue, just the fact that so many people had no trouble believing it showed that Lombardi's legend had taken root. You don't mess with the "Old Man."

But the battles, both big and small, were taking a toll on him and by the end of the '67 season, he was worn out physically, emotionally—every way imaginable.

Kramer often compared Lombardi in those final years in Green Bay to a president of the United States who had come into office bright-eyed and enthusiastic but who after several years looked as though he aged a decade.

"In 1967 he looked that way," Kramer recalled. "He looked gray and he looked tired."

Amazingly, from the time Lombardi ran off the field in triumph after beating the Cowboys on that frozen December afternoon, the great coach would live only two-and-a-half more years.

In September 1970, after battling colon cancer for months (though in truth symptoms, ignored and derided, had been evident for several years) Lombardi died at age fifty-seven. Thousands, including many of his former players, attended with many still in shock that something had cut down the seemingly indestructible Lombardi.

His end came too soon for so many. In a different way, the same can be said for Tom Landry.

He was the Dallas Cowboys. From top to bottom and from inside and out, he was the franchise, the message, the team, the attitude, the success, and the failures.

Landry was the first head coach of the Cowboys. And there was a time no one ever really thought there would be another.

For twenty-nine seasons, Landry walked the sidelines, as hard to read as Sanskrit and as unknowable as quantum physics. In today's NFL, which demands instant success immediately, Landry likely would not have survived the team's early struggles.

Though he was building a dynasty, it was being constructed at a painful slow pace—adding a running back one season, a linebacker the next, a left tackle the next. Landry knew greatness was not constructed overnight and his Cowboys were proof of that.

After all, it took six seasons for the Cowboys to even post a .500 record. But when they went 10–3–1 the following season, and earned a shot at the NFL title against the Packers, they would not have a losing season again for twenty years. They would reach the playoffs eighteen times, winning thirteen division titles and two Super Bowls.

And while his methods rubbed many players the wrong way, none of them could argue about the results.

One long-time Packer, defensive back Herb Adderley, left Green Bay in 1970 and played his final three seasons with the Cowboys. And while he enjoyed success on the field, Landry's hands-off approach left him frustrated. Sure, he said, Lombardi would yell all the time but at least you knew where you stood with him. Landry? He was an enigma to many players.

Then, after the Cowboys dipped to 7–9 in 1986, their first losing season since 1964, the whispers began about Tom Landry. The NFL had changed and it had left Landry behind, the critics chirped.

Of course, the irony wasn't lost on others. This was the coach who changed the concept of NFL defenses, had refined the shotgun offense, had sent flankers in motion and dominated the NFL for two decades and now could not adapt to an NFL that put a premium on passing?

It seemed ridiculous. But then came the strike-interrupted 1987 season and again the Cowboys looked slow and unprepared. A 7–8 record followed.

The whispers had now become full-throated criticism and by 1988, the Cowboys were spinning out of control. A 3–13 record stunned not only Cowboys fans but the entire NFL. What had happened to the gold standard of professional football? They had been passed by faster, slicker, more complex teams such as the San Francisco 49ers and Washington Redskins and the Cowboys had been left behind.

Some old-time Cowboys saw what was happening and were dismayed. They saw a team that was undisciplined and disinterested and old. Privately, and not so privately, they suggested that Landry was holding on to players who could no longer do the job out of some sense of loyalty.

That was really the first time the unthinkable became all-too-possible. Maybe the game really had left the sixty-four-year-old Landry behind. The players were faster, stronger, probably smarter, and they surely did not take to the only kind of coaching Landry knew.

Maybe, after twenty-nine seasons, it was time for him to step away. His old friend and rival Vince Lombardi had lasted in the Packers pressure cooker for only nine seasons. Landry had roamed the Cowboys sideline and maintained a staggering standard three times longer than that. The man had coached one team for nearly three decades.

Landry, a proud and emotional man even though he spent a lifetime keeping it under wraps from the public, heard the criticism and was defiant.

"I will coach for as long as I think I can do the job," he said after the disastrous 1988 season. "Or until someone tells me I can't."

That someone was on the horizon and closing fast.

At the same time the Cowboys were hitting rock bottom, a brash Arkansas oilman, Jerry Jones, purchased the Cowboys and Texas Stadium from owner H. R. "Bum" Bright for $140 million. Jones wanted to reestablish the Cowboys as the so-called America's Team, a title it had lost in recent years.

And the first step, he thought, was making a clean break with the past.

In February, 1989, in a move he now regrets in the severity and speed in which it occurred, Jones fired Landry and replaced him with his old football teammate at the University of Arkansas, the equally brash and mercurial Jimmy Johnson, who had built a consistent powerhouse at the University of Miami.

It was a thunderous and tone-deaf move by Jones and left Cowboys fans reeling. Yes, perhaps it was time for Landry to be replaced. But not like this. Not unlike Lombardi, he had given his life to the Cowboys and to be brushed away so unceremoniously was simply cruel.

Landry took his dismissal in typically stoic fashion, but inside he seethed. But a few days later, when he said goodbye to his players, Landry wept.

In recent years, Jones admits he botched that decision and in retrospect would have kept Landry at least another season until the new owner had a sense of how the organization worked.

Indeed, in Johnson's first season, with a host of new players and with a roster that would be almost entirely rebuilt, the Cowboys staggered to a 1–15 record. But two years later Johnson would have the Cowboys back in the playoffs and they would be Super Bowl champs in 1992, 1993, and 1995.

Of course, in the time since Jones purchased the team, there have also seven head coaches and no trip backs to the Super Bowl since those three.

Landry and the love of his life, Alicia, slipped into the shadows, remaining in Dallas. He was inducted into the Pro Football Hall of Fame in 1990 and earned a spot in the Cowboys Ring of Honor in 1993. It was the last time he was in Texas Stadium.

In 1999, Landry was diagnosed with leukemia and in February of 2000 he passed away. Years later, his widow Alicia said her husband had died a New York Giants fan.

Is there a good way for any head coach to leave the game they love so much? Some are lucky and can retire when they know deep in their bones it's time to walk away. But most do not.

Vince Lombardi could have coached the Packers for as long as he chose to but he knew his time in Green Bay was over. He saw the team he built growing old and he did not have the strength or inclination to build another one. He did have one more season of coaching, a thoroughly satisfying one with the rebuilding Washington Redskins in 1969. But his health gave out and he had just the one season.

He remarked to several former players from his hospital bedthat if he'd had a quarterback in Green Bay like the Redskins' Sonny Jurgensen, his Packers never would have lost a game.

Landry's dismissal was even more hurtful and he resented Jerry Jones until the day he died.

"But," he said, "I can't worry about things over which I have no control," he said.

Vince Lombardi and Tom Landry are still tied together over the decades. Indeed, maybe neither would have been as successful as they were if they didn't have the other pushing them. But each created a team for the ages.

"Both teams were pretty damn good," said Cowboys linebacker Lee Roy Jordan. "The thing is we lost two championship games to Green Bay. If we win those maybe the Super Bowl trophy isn't called the Lombardi Trophy, maybe it's called the Tom Landry Trophy."

4

THE RIVALRY

THE DALLAS COWBOYS were born in chaos.

It was 1960 and professional football found itself expanding in ways even it hadn't even considered. The game had taken off with the American public, slowing but inexorably gaining on baseball, the game that Americans had embraced for decades.

There was a thirst for the game that the National Football League seemed able and willing to quench.

Indeed, it had seemed so simple for so many years. The NFL had the run of the neighborhood since its formation. It had begun, really, in 1919, when a group of businessmen in the Midwest had seen football as a game with national appeal and with the hubris and financial wherewithal to take their dream to the next level.

It was originally known as the American Professional Football Association and featured teams in such places as Akron, Ohio, Rock Island, Illinois, and Canton, Ohio.

There was also a team in a little Wisconsin town of Green Bay that was known as the Acme Packers who were formed by local star athlete Curly Lambeau and George Calhoun, sports editor of the local newspaper.

It was fragile conglomeration of teams, with egos and disputes dominating the landscape. In fact, the Packers lost their franchise in 1921 because they had used illegal players and they'd been ratted out by the owner of the franchise in Decatur, Illinois, a fellow named George Halas.

But by 1922, everything was changing.

The Packers, now renamed the Green Bay Packers, had returned, the Decatur franchise moved to Chicago now known as the Bears and several of the smaller franchises had dropped off. The collection of pro teams was renamed the National Football League and for decades, it would be the only game in town.

There had been other rivals, such as the All-America Football Conference, but the NFL had set its sights on making sure it did not succeed—and it didn't.

But in 1960, the world was changing. The hunger for pro football was growing and expanding beyond the borders where the NFL had franchises. Suddenly, there was a burning interest for teams, especially in the South and West.

And a new group of businessmen, flush with cash and an interest in challenging the NFL, had appeared.

This group saw opportunities, and had the resources, to make it work. They called their new league the American Football League and, armed with a new TV contract, it was ready to compete.

And, for the first time in years, the NFL was taking notice because they saw the AFL as a serious challenge to their power.

The AFL featured teams in Los Angeles and Denver and Oakland and Houston as well as East Coast spots such as New York, Buffalo, and Boston.

One of those new AFL teams was also be situated in Dallas, Texas, a growing city perfect for the AFL's southern strategy and where football was already hugely popular.

The Dallas AFL franchise would be called the Texans and was bankrolled by a bright young Texas oilman, Lamar Hunt, who had desperately tried to secure a franchise in the NFL but was rebuffed.

So he did the next best thing and formed the new AFL (there had been three earlier leagues with that name that failed) and his entry into the new league would be another thumb in the eye of the autocrats of the NFL.

Stunned by the move, the NFL decided it needed to do something it had not done in years—expand. And to combat the AFL's move into the south, the NFL focused on putting a team of its own in Dallas. It would be owned by Clint Murchison, a Texan who had hard feelings of his own toward the NFL.

Murchison had expected to join forces with what at the time had been the southernmost team in the NFL, the Washington Redskins, and its mercurial owner George Preston Marshall. But the sale of the Redskins to Murchison, with Marshall staying on for a few years to run the team never panned out, and it later became clear to Marshall that his opposition to a Dallas team in the NFL would be counterproductive.

So on January 28, 1960, Dallas was approved for an NFL franchise. After going through two possible team names—Steers and Rangers—the Cowboys was at last settled on and a new coach, a defensive assistant coach who had worked wonders with the New York Giants, was hired.

That was Tom Landry.

The Cowboys, made up castoffs and wannabes, struggled in those early years, going 0–11–1 in their first season and failing to post a winning record until 1966. But the NFL had made its point to the upstart AFL.

The two pro football teams in town shared a home stadium at the Cotton Bowl and the NFL, with more resources, began to overwhelm the Texans. And even the though the Texas won the AFL title in 1962, Hunt could see the writing on the wall. In 1963, he moved his franchise to Kansas City and renamed it the Chiefs where it has enjoyed success ever since.

And Dallas became an NFL city once and for all.

Also, early in 1960 in a location about as far removed from Dallas, Texas, as a community could be, fans of Green Bay Packers were beginning to have reason to hope again.

Vince Lombardi, who had teamed up with Landry in New York and coordinated the Giants' offense, had just completed his first season as head coach in 1959 and he posted a 7–5 record, the Packers' first winning season since 1947.

The next season, he'd lead the Packers to the NFL Championship Game where they would fall to the Philadelphia Eagles. That was where Lombardi made his now famous pronouncement after that loss that no longer would a team of his lose a championship game. And they didn't.

There was no rivalry between the Cowboys and the Packers at that time. How could there be? The Packers were, for lack of a better term, NFL royalty. One of the original teams who had already produced some of the most legendary players the game had seen—Curly Lambeau, Don Hutson, Mike Michalske, Cal Hubbard, Johnny "Blood" McNally, Clarke Hinkle—and had already won six NFL titles.

The Cowboys were starting from scratch but Landry knew, if they built the right way, there was no reason his Cowboys couldn't one day be where the Packers were.

The first meeting between the two franchises came in Dallas's inaugural season in 1960 and it went as everyone expected it should have. The methodical, powerful Packers blasted the young Cowboys, 41–7, forcing five turnovers and rolling up 391 total yards.

The two teams didn't meet again until 1964, but the result was no different. The Packers forced six turnovers, including fumble returns for touchdowns by Lionel Aldridge and Henry Jordan, and won, 45–21.

But when they met again the next season, a change was in the air. By 1965, much of the roster that would challenge the Packers for the NFL title in 1966 and again in 1967 was in place.

On offense, there was quarterback Don Meredith, fullback Don Perkins, halfback Dan Reeves, and wide receiver Bob Hayes and a formidable defense led by tackles Jethro Pugh and Bob Lilly, linebackers Dave Edwards and Chuck Howley, and defense back Mel Renfro were established.

And in a rugged October affair at Milwaukee County Stadium, the Packers stayed unbeaten with a 13–3 win. But the Cowboys sent a message, holding quarterback Bart Starr to four completions in 19 attempts and allowing the Packers only 63 total yards.

On offense, Perkins ran for 133 yards against the Packers' proud defense, but the Cowboys also committed five turnovers, which led to the loss.

Still, the Cowboys had seen what they needed to see. They had outplayed the eventual NFL champs on their home turf, and they had done it with tough defense and an offense that, when it wasn't turning the ball over, could compete with anyone.

The pieces were in place.

In 1966, the Cowboys were in their seventh year of existence. They had made steady, unspectacular improvement, but it had been improvement nonetheless.

Tom Landry had put together a team that was beginning to reflect who he was as a person and as a coach, not unlike the man who was guiding the Packers.

Landry wanted his teams to be professional and smart. He was not an emotional person and he didn't want his players to be either. After all, he believed that emotion is fleeting and unreliable. Players, he believed, could only rely on emotion for so long during a game. Then it would dissipate and all that would remain was talent and preparation.

And he continued to look at the Packers as the template to win the right way. They were pros from one end of the roster to the other and in the previous four meetings against Green Bay, his players had made critical mistakes at the worst time. The Packers had not.

But this was the season when is young, talented players had enough NFL experience to take the next step.

The Cowboys roared through the regular season with a 10–3–1 record, the best in team history. They led the league in points scored and, more important, they had a defense for the ages, nicknamed the "Doomsday Defense." Deep down Landry loved the nickname but he'd never let anyone, especially his players, know it.

They had proven themselves in the regular season but now came real challenge, the real test as to whether they had moved into the upper levels of the NFL.

The Cowboys were in the playoffs for the first time and would host their nemesis, the Packers, for the NFL championship. Green Bay was already the defending NFL champions, having beaten the Cleveland Browns the season before. Now they were back with a 12–2 record and looking at a chance to win back-to-back titles.

On the surface, it appeared the Packers would dominate the young Cowboys, who had only one starting player over the age of thirty, linebacker Chuck Howley.

But this game had a different feel for other reasons. After all, this would be the first year that the NFL championship would not mean what it usually meant. Heading into the 1967 season, the dominant NFL and the relentless AFL both realized that there was no advantage for either in continuing to wage war against each other, whether it was for money or personnel or territorial rights.

So the team leagues agreed to merge, eventually melding into one league, the National Football League, with two conferences, the NFC and the AFC.

But that would take a few years. In the meantime, the two leagues agreed to hold a true "world championship," pitting the best of the NFL against the top AFL team. It would be called the Super Bowl and, in time, it would become the biggest sporting event in America. Or at least that was the hope of those involved.

The Cowboys couldn't have been more excited. This was their first opportunity to prove on a national stage that they belonged with the big boys. For the Packers, it was yet another challenge from another up and coming team that felt it had what it took to dethrone the champs.

But the Packers also knew that even if they won another NFL title, there was now another game awaiting them, against an unfamiliar foe.

On top of that, there were persistent rumors that Vince Lombardi was thinking about stepping down as head coach.

And then there was the opponent itself. The Dallas Cowboys, at least in the view of many, were the future of the NFL. Lombardi knew Landry all too well and while he was loathe to throw around the term "genius," he knew very few coaches who could construct and run a defense the way Landry could. He had seen it in New York when they both assistant coaches and he had seen it in Dallas, with his innovative and difficult "flex" defense.

This would be no cakewalk, Lombardi knew.

First, he knew that Landry would spend much of his time looking to slow down Green Bay's vaunted sweep. It was not a complicated play; it was never meant to be. But over the years, the Packers had run it with such intricate perfection that it had become part of NFL lore.

It was the play Lombardi demanded to be run correctly all the time because it was the play that would be his team's signature of dominance.

It was a play that demanded the guard and tackle get out of their three-point stances quickly, get to the corner and deliver blocks that would spring backs that, over the years, featured Hall of Famers Paul Hornung and Jim Taylor and, later, Elijah Pitts, Donny Anderson, and Jim Grabowski. The linemen who triggered the sweep were the likes of guards Fuzzy Thurston and Jerry Kramer and tackle Forrest Gregg.

And for rival defenders, it was a daunting sight.

Lem Barney, the wonderful cornerback for the Detroit Lions, saw that sweep more times than he cared to think about.

He laughed when asked what he thought when he saw it coming.

"I'd say, 'Hail Mary, full of grace the Lord is with thee,'" he said. "It was a fearsome thing to see."

The Cowboys' defense, of course, knew all about it.

"Everybody in the league did it," said tackle Bob Lilly, "just not as good as the Packers."

Linebacker Lee Roy Jordan had been amazed at the Packers' brutal simplicity on offense.

"They ran just a few plays but they ran them to perfection," he said. "Everybody had an assignment and I guarantee you, coach Lombardi made sure everybody did them."

So as they prepared to meet the Packers in 1966, the Cowboys knew if they could shut down what the Packers did best, they could be beaten.

In fact, to understand the dramatic game that would unfold just a year later in Green Bay, it is important to understand this first championship meeting in Dallas.

Bob Long, an underrated Packers receiver in those days, told Gary D'Amato of the *Milwaukee Journal Sentinel* in 2017 that game has been overlooked by history but shouldn't be.

"I tell people if you want to analyze all the great games in NFL history, you have to include that game in the Cotton Bowl," he said. "[Linebacker] Dave Robinson and I get together all the time and we talk about that game. That was one game that I really think back upon. The fans might not talk about it much but the players still do, I can tell you that. We remember."

It was the type of game that should have been played in 1967 but, due to circumstances beyond anyone's control, it was not.

It was Lombardi and Landry at their finest, with each utilizing their skills the best way they knew how.

Lombardi knew enough about what Landry planned and, while practicing in Tulsa, Oklahoma the week before the game, he showed he hadn't lost his ability to surprise. Despite an unexpected ice storm during their practice week, Lombardi was still able to concoct a scheme that he felt would at least surprise the Cowboys defense, if not stop it.

Landry had remembered from his days coaching with Lombardi in New York that Lombardi hated when his offense was made to look bad. So Landry, with his innovative new "flex" defense, had a perfect opportunity to make that happen. All they needed were a few breaks.

But, like a poker player who instinctively knew the hand of his opponents, Lombardi was ready to gamble. The Packers would use just a few plays, run perfectly, on offense. But instead of brute force and power, he would have his offense use misdirection, something the Packers usually shied away from, and play-action passes in ways he rarely did.

Landry, confident Lombardi would do something to surprise his team, believed his team was ready.

It was two coaches at the top of their game who had shaped their teams, into playing at their highest levels. It would prove to be a memorable game not many people remember.

"We were not intimidated by the Packers," said Cowboys cornerback Mel Renfro. "As a matter of fact we felt very strongly that we were the better team."

Indeed, in a theme that would continue the next season, the Packers entered that game banged up and limping. The great rushing attack that had made the Packers so fearsome the previous few seasons was struggling that year.

Fullback Jim Taylor and halfbacks Elijah Pitts and Paul Hornung all battled injuries in 1966 and they still were not 100 percent for the playoffs. So Lombardi decided to scrap his infamous power sweep and allow Bart Starr to throw the ball.

No one in the NFL was ever especially intimidated by Starr's throwing ability. But what he could do was manage a game and win. No one knew that better than the Cowboys defense.

"He was an astute quarterback," recalled linebacker Lee Roy Jordan. "He'd use audibles when he thought he had the advantage. He was always prepared and a great leader. He managed the team and he never made a mistake. And he was underrated as a quarterback. I mean, he has five championship so that should say something."

So the decision was simple. With a struggling running game, the Packers would live or die with the passing game.

"Coach Lombardi, his philosophy was to take what the defense gives you," wide receiver Carroll Dale told Gary D'Amato. "If they came up eight in the box, he would throw on every down if he needed to."

Ironically, it was a misdirection running play, put in that week and which the Dallas defense had not seen before, that got the Packers rolling on their first possession of the game.

Pitts broke free for a 32-yard run on the opening play and later on the same drive, he scored on a 17-yard pass from Starr.

Mel Renfro fumbled the ensuing kickoff and Green Bay's Jim Grabowski returned it 18 yards to give Green Bay a 14–0 lead before Dallas's first play.

"I returned kicks for several years and that's the only time I ever fumbled," Renfro recalled.

The quick strike stunned everyone, especially a young team trying to gain its bearings in the most important game it had ever played.

"They jumped off to such a big lead," Reeves recalled. "I don't know if you could tell that much difference between the two teams. They still had great players. We knew they were a veteran football team that wasn't going to beat themselves."

For the Cowboys, it was time to demonstrate what they could do in the toughest circumstances they could imagine. And for their often maligned quarterback Don Meredith, that's exactly the way he wanted it.

So down two touchdowns before they'd even run a play, Meredith stepped in the offensive huddle with his shaken young team and did what he always did best.

"Folks, we're in a heap of shit," he said.

Center Dave Manders also remembers that Meredith came into the huddle and smiled.

"He looks over at the referee, I think it was Tommy Bell, and says, 'Hey Tommy, I need a timeout,'" Manders said. "Bell says, 'You can't call a timeout until you run a play.' So just like that Don looks at our right tackle Ralph Neely and says, 'Hey Ralph, look over at the 25-yard-line. Isn't that the girl you were with last night? How was it?"

The Cowboys huddle erupted in laughter.

"Don turns to Bell and says, 'OK, Tommy we're ready to play,'" Manders said. "That's exactly what we needed. It calmed us down. But that's what Don did. People don't know how smart that guy was. He had like a 175 IQ. He was a smart guy and always knew what he was doing."

That break did indeed settle the Cowboys down and they immediately responded with a 13-play scoring drive that ended with 3-yard touchdown run by Dan Reeves. After a Packers punt, the Cowboys drove again and tied the game on a 23-yard touchdown run by fullback Don Perkins.

And so it would go for the rest of the game. Two evenly matched team pounding away on each other in a game most observers saw as the real championship of pro football.

Packers backup quarterback Zeke Bratkowski remembers the Packers game plan was nothing dramatic but was being executed as well as he'd ever seen it.

"We had probably the best game plan I've ever seen and we executed it extremely well," he said. "The things we did, we did very well."

And much of it settled on the shoulders of Starr, who may not have had Meredith's swagger, but had the experience and patience to do the job.

The two teams battled back and forth but it seemed Green Bay seemed to have taken control in the fourth quarter when Starr threw a 28-yard touchdown pass to Max McGee on third down. Bob Lilly blocked the extra point so the Packers led 34–20.

The defense needed a stop but couldn't get it.

With five minutes to play, Dallas rallied again, scoring on a 68-yard touchdown pass from Meredith to Frank Clarke, who had dominated Packers safety Tom Brown all day.

When Green Bay was unable to run out the clock, the Cowboys got one more chance to at least tie the game and send it to overtime. And in overtime, anything could happen.

"We really thought we were going to score," recalled halfback Dan Reeves. "We never even considered that we wouldn't."

With barely three minutes remaining in the game and a Cotton Bowl crowd roaring in the background, the Cowboys rolled to the Green Bay 22-yard line.

A pass interference penalty on the battered and beaten Brown gave the Cowboys a first down at the Packers 2-yard line.

With the ball at the 1, tackle Jim Boeke committed a devastating five-yard false start penalty, moving the ball back to the 6.

Reeves, who had had his eye scratched earlier on the drive, dropped a pass that might resulted in the tying touchdown.

But eventually, the Cowboys faced 4th-and-goal from the Green Bay 1 and when Meredith rolled right looking for Bob Hayes in the end zone, Meredith was greeted in the backfield by linebacker Dave Robinson.

Ignoring his assignment that told him to remain in coverage, Robinson saw the opportunity to disrupt Meredith and force a bad throw. In fact, Robinson took advantage of an uncharacteristic Landry mistake. Normally on the play called in that situation, flanker Bob Hayes came out of the game in favor of the stronger Frank Clarke. But Hayes, an indifferent blocker at best, missed his assignment, which was Dave Robinson.

With Robinson draped all over him, Meredith got off a wobbly sidearm pass that was intercepted in the back of the end zone by Brown, a gift for him after a long, difficult day.

And on the sideline, the normally stoic and implacable Landry, who believed emotion was a waste in pursuit of victory, looked away and grimaced. It was the reaction of a coach who knew a great opportunity had slipped away and there was no guarantee it would ever come again.

The Packers held on for the 34–27 win and realized only after the game that another remained— an historic meeting with the AFL champion Kansas City Chiefs.

But that was for another day and another time.

That NFL Championship Game, which has never received the notoriety it deserved especially after what happened the following year, was perhaps Bart Starr's greatest performance.

He played superbly against the Cowboys, completing 19 of 28 passes for 304 yards, throwing four touchdowns and no interceptions.

And if fans didn't appreciate it, the guys on the field that night did.

"I don't think there's any question that Bart is in the top ten, maybe top five, of quarterbacks all time," Renfro said. "Bart has to rank among the best."

Bill Curry, who was Green Bay's center in 1965 and '66 before being traded to the Baltimore Colts, never lost his respect for the quarterback, who took more hits that anyone ever knew.

"For me it was like putting my head in the huddle and seeing Mount Rushmore," he said. "I wasn't going to let anyone touch him. I'll tackle them if I have to. With Bart, it was like being in the presence of God. If I ever displeased him, I was crushed."

"In my opinion, he was the most accurate quarterback of all time," said receiver Bob Long.

Meredith, despite battling injury, also played well, completing 15 of 31 passes for 238 yards with one touchdown and one decisive interception. Perkins rushed for 108 yards and a score, while Reeves rushed for 47 yards, caught four passes for 77 yards, and scored a touchdown.

Afterward, Lombardi was more jubilant than his players expected him to be though he sought out Robinson after the game and, after congratulating him for the game-saving play, scolded him for breaking his assignment. In Lombardi's complex defensive grading system, Robinson would have to be marked down for the mistake.

"I didn't care," Robinson said with a smile.

This win was special and Lombardi knew it. He had taken on his old friend, and rival, from the New York Giants and come out on top. Lombardi could see the future and he saw this Cowboys team that Landry had put together as the embodiment of that. It was a team that would be very good for a long time.

But for now, his Packers still reigned supreme. It was the first real test between the reigning NFL champs and the newcomers who wanted to take over that title.

"We played really well that game but Green Bay did just enough to beat us," Reeves said. "We knew then what we had to do to get better."

Bob Lilly looked at the loss as an opportunity lost.

"They never made any major errors," said Lilly, who had joined the Cowboys in the early days when no one really knew if Landry's ambition building plan would ultimately work. "They always played a pretty simple offense but they had a few special plays and they were very timely about using them. They were just very professional."

Of course, a year later, in the arctic conditions of Green Bay, an eerily similar situation would unfold. Facing fourth down and goal from the Cowboys' 1, the Packers had to score or lose. The Cowboys' coaching staff afterward was convinced Starr would roll out and try to throw for a touchdown, just as Meredith had done at the Cotton Bowl.

Instead, Starr kept the ball, scored, and made the Ice Bowl part of NFL history.

After beating the Cowboys in 1966, the Packers went on to beat the AFL champion Kansas City Chiefs, but Lombardi, and every Packers player, knew the real championship had been played in the Cotton Bowl two weeks earlier.

"We knew that was a good team,' linebacker Ray Nitschke said of the Cowboys.

After surviving the Ice Bowl in 1967, the Packers again beat the AFL's best, the Oakland Raiders, to win Super Bowl II.

But the NFL hierarchy was changing.

In 1968, the Packers, under the direction of a new coach in Phil Bengtson, were a year older and year more banged up, yet they still managed to beat the Cowboys for the sixth straight time, 28–17, in a regular season game in Dallas.

The lessons continued that day as the Cowboys, who had been 6–0 coming into the game, committed four turnovers. Starr was again terrific, throwing for four touchdowns, while Meredith struggled, throwing three interceptions.

But change could not be stopped.

The Cowboys went 12–2 that season and lost to Cleveland in the playoffs. The Packers finished 6–7–1 and missed the playoffs for only the fourth time since 1959.

Finally in 1970, the Cowboys beat their nemesis, holding the Packers to 129 total yards in a 16–3 regular season win. That was also the season when the Cowboys reached the Super Bowl for the first time, falling to the Baltimore Colts.

Over the course of the next forty-five years, the two teams would lock horns twenty-eight times, including six in the post-season, with the Cowboys holding a 16–12 advantage. There have been upsets and there have been blowouts and there has been controversy.

And in all that time and over all those games, the phrase *Ice Bowl* was uttered just once— when the Packers hosted the Cowboys in the 2014 divisional playoffs. Amazingly, it was the first time the two long-time rivals had met in a playoff game at Lambeau Field since that day so many years earlier when survival was the order of the day.

And, of course, the national media, which had grown dramatically in the four decades since the Ice Bowl, wanted to make it something resembling Ice Bowl II.

But a temperature of 24 degrees at game time and a wind chill of a balmy zero for the January 11, 2015, game made any comparisons pointless. Green Bay won that day, 26–21, and instead of wind chills and frostbite, the topic of the day was what constituted a reception in today's NFL as a fourth-down grab by Dez Bryant of the Cowboys at the Green Bay 1-yard line was overturned and ruled not to be a catch.

In terms of blood rivals, the Green Bay Packers and their fans can still point proudly to the Chicago Bears and Minnesota Vikings. But the Cowboys remain high on the list.

And one Cowboy who played a major role in the Ice Bowl is convinced that having played the Packers in those formative years was a turning point for the franchise.

"I remember we lost to Cleveland the next two years in the playoffs [after the Ice Bowl] but I was convinced the Packers were better than those Browns teams we lost to," Reeves said. "And I'm not sure we would have had that much success without having played the Packers and learned how to play the game the right way. We always tried to do that because we learned that from the Packers."

5

THE FANS

OFFICIALLY, THE 1967 NFL Championship Game was listed as a sellout. In truth nobody really knows how many fans actually showed up. Those were the days when turnstiles were still considered high tech and no-shows were simply the folks who didn't show up in the seat next to you.

Of course, to hear Packers fans tell the story, either they attended the Ice Bowl or their parents or grandparents or aunts and uncles or third cousins or close friend were there. Somebody everyone knew, it seemed, was there.

It's a joke told by many Packers and Cowboys players and not quickly denied by fans, those who were there and those who were not. It's one of the great tales told by Packers fans, a devoted group that will tell you everything you want to know about their team, whether you want to know or not.

It's also one of the great fables told by Packers fans who want to make it clear than that, even in those days, when protection from the elements meant wearing an additional pair of gloves, that for fans in Green Bay, the game matters most. The weather? An incidental part of the festivities and, besides, it could have been colder.

Even today, players who took part in the game marvel at the people who showed up.

"I still can't imagine playing in a game like that," said Cowboys linebacker Lee Roy Jordan. "Can you imagine seventeen below zero? Most of the fans there had something to keep them warm. They had alcohol. I thought someone was going to offer us some but no one ever did."

"We were pretty uncomfortable," said Cowboys defensive tackle Bob Lilly.

But in its retelling over the ocean of time, this much is certain: the official attendance for the NFL Championship Game on December 31, 1967 was 50,861, the capacity of Lambeau Field at the time. That means every ticket available was purchased but no one, not even the most diehard of diehard Packers fans, believe every seat was taken that day.

Best estimates from those who really were there that day seem to suggest that there were probably 2,000 to 3,000 fans that simply could not make it due to transportation issues, lack of motivation or, perhaps, common sense. More fans left during the game as the temperature continued to drop and the football field turned from simply slick to all but unplayable. But make no mistake, by the end of the game, the stadium was still rollicking.

Remember, these were the days when fans couldn't just stay home and watch their heroes on the flat screen. The NFL strictly controlled the airwaves and home games were blacked out in NFL cities. That meant Green Bay viewers were out of luck.

So most stayed—out of loyalty; out of the need to follow through on what they started; out of the belief that their Packers would somehow find a way to prevail.

"Lambeau Field was really something special and we always knew how tough they were to play there," said Jordan. "It was a great home-field advantage they had, and it was a great home-field crowd. It was unbelievably vibrant. Even in the cold weather, they'd clap with their gloves on. They were very devoted fans and the Packers always played well in front of them."

Even when the Packers struggled in the 1940s and '50s, sellout crowds at Packers games were nothing unusual. This was their team, good or bad, though it was mostly bad for a long time.

Lambeau Field in 1967 was a classic college-style bowl with none of the amenities of modern NFL stadiums. And if there are unsung heroes for that day, it was the fans who stayed to the bitterly cold end and saw history.

The stadium had been built in 1957, seated 32,000 and was called City Stadium. Vice President Richard Nixon was on hand to officially open the new stadium, and the Packers did their part by beating the hated Chicago Bears.

They would not win there again that season though in 1958, the worst season in team history, their only win all year was secured in a home game against the Philadelphia Eagles. Home-field advantage? Not in Green Bay. At least not yet.

But in 1959, a new coach had stepped in, and everything started to change. In his first game in charge, Vince Lombardi's new team beat the Bears again. In fact, they'd start the season with a 3–0 home record and end a 7–5 season with a 4–2 home mark.

It was a start, at least.

In 1961, the stadium was expanded again, this time to 38,000 seats and in 1963, 4,000 more seats were added.

In 1965, the stadium was expanded to nearly 51,000 and, more important, it was renamed Lambeau Field in honor of the team's founder and first coach. It was a move that angered Lombardi, who felt Lambeau did not deserve the honor due to his well-known extramarital shenanigans and the way he and the team had split so acrimoniously fifteen years earlier. There was talk in more than a few corners that Lombardi was angry because he had hoped, one day, the stadium would be named for him.

By that point, the Packers had become a dominant team, whether it was in Green Bay or at its home away from home, Milwaukee County Stadium. Since 1919, the Packers had played at least two games a season in Milwaukee, as a way to say thank you to Milwaukee fans for helping the team survive its early years.

Starting in 1953, the Packers would play at least two games a season in the quirky Milwaukee County Stadium, which had been built for baseball. Cramped and uncomfortable and haunted by some terrible sight lines for many fans, the most curious part of the part of playing there was that the two teams shared the same sideline.

But the Packers were successful there, too, even playing a first-round playoff game in 1967 season and beating the Los Angeles Rams a week before the Ice Bowl.

It wasn't until 1994, when Lambeau Field had again been expanded and more expansion was anticipated, made the decision to stop playing in Milwaukee. Fans in the southern part of the state were furious but eventually were placated when the Packers offered a three-game Lambeau Field package to Milwaukee fans. It has worked seamlessly since.

But whether playing in Green Bay or in Milwaukee, Lombardi demanded his teams protect their home turf. Both venues were unusual and distinct and not just for the changeable weather. Packers fans were loyal and vocal and obsessed with their team, the fans knew better than anyone how unusual and special it was for a town of that size to have an NFL franchise.

It was a quirk of fate and luck and timing and circumstances that Green Bay was still in the NFL at all and more than a few times team officials would hear from owners of teams in larger cities (and sometimes the media which covered those teams) that Green Bay did not belong with the big boys.

In truth, it was becoming hard for men like team president Dominic Olejniczak to make a good case for the Packers' existence, especially in those years in the '40s and '50s when the team was terrible and, for a lack of a better term, merely taking up space in a league that was clearly exploding in popularity. A bad team in a small town? Was there a better recipe for relocation?

So when the Packers hired Lombardi, who had no head coaching experience, it as a gamble of monumental proportions. The fans might stick around but, just maybe, more losing and no signs it would get any better, could keep even the NFL's most loyal fans at home.

But Lombardi won fans over quickly. They liked his New York bravado, his emotion, his passion, his ability to get everything he could out of his players. And, of course, they loved the fact in his first game as head coach, the Packers beat the hated Chicago Bears.

In his nine seasons as Green Bay's head coach, the Packers posted a 32–8–1 record at City Stadium/Lambeau Field, including the Ice Bowl and playoff wins over the New York Giants, Cleveland Browns, and Baltimore Colts. At Milwaukee County Stadium, the Packers were even better, winning 20 of 25 games in that span, including the playoff win over the Rams.

The NFL Championship Game on December 31, 1967, when the temperature fell into places few even in Wisconsin had seen before, would be the last postseason contest hosted by the Packers until January 8, 1983, when they played the St. Louis Cardinals as part of the strike-shortened 1982 season "playoff tournament."

It was, of course, a sellout and a celebration but it was also a realization on the part of many Packers that it had been too long and that, if history was any guide, it might be years again before Lambeau saw a playoff game.

But as fans streamed into Lambeau Field to watch the Packers play the Cowboys in 1967, the future was someone else's problem. The Packers were playing for another championship, and the temperature could be 50 below with howling winds and snow—the fans would be there because that's what Packers fans did.

That image never left Cowboys players.

Players remember looking into the stands and seeing clouds of mists rising from the combination of frosty breath and cigarette smoke. It was a surreal image that reminded many players of some arctic wasteland.

Even today, Lilly, the Hall of Fame defensive tackle, talks with something akin to reverence of the people who came to a game that fans from other cities wouldn't have attended on a bet. But this was Green Bay.

"I had a great deal of admiration for everyone who went," he recalled. "I thought, 'These people are tough.' I remember there were three guys behind us, the third or fourth row up, wearing no shorts or coats or anything and they were drinking out of a pint bottle so that answered a few questions for me. And this was before the game even started. I told [defensive end] George Andrie, 'Those guys are going to die.' I remember I looked up there during the game and those guys were gone. I wondered if those guys had died. Turns out they put their coats on. Still pretty impressive though."

Gil Brandt, the Cowboys' general manager at the time, had been shaken by the news the morning of the game that the temperature has gone through the floor and the game would be played in below zero temperatures.

He recalled that as the teams went through the oxymoron of "warming up" an hour or so before game time, the stadium was all but empty.

"There wasn't a person in the stands," Brandt said years later. "It was completely empty. When we went back in the locker room, it was still completely empty."

The Cowboys weren't that surprised. After all, who would come in that kind of weather to watch a football game? It made no sense to them. Indeed, many expected, when told the game would be played, believed it would played in that same empty environs except, perhaps, for a few die-hards. It would be the strangest setting they'd ever been involved in—at least that's what they expected.

But a funny thing happened.

When the Cowboys came back out of their locker room to prepare for the game, everything had changed.

"When we came back out five or six minutes before kickoff, there wasn't an empty seat in the place," Brandt said. "Amazing."

The Packers players were less surprised by what they witnessed from their fans. They knew these people. They saw them all the time, knew what they capable of, and understood the way others did not that football was too important to them to let a little frostbite get in the way.

"Best fans in football," quarterback Bart Starr said afterward.

Over the years, rumors swirled about what happened in the stands at Lambeau Field during the Ice Bowl. For years, it was believed eight to ten people died from exposure. One man supposedly slipped on ice and broke his neck.

But as the years went by and reality gave way to the great stories, it seems none of this was true. One elderly man did die from a heart attack. But as far as numerous fatalities brought on by staggering cold, it simply was shown not to be true.

There were plenty of cases of frostbite and more than a few people missed work that week due to illness that probably came from sitting in sub-zero cold for three hours. And in those days, while it was frowned upon for fans to bring in alcoholic beverages into the stadium, no one took it all that seriously. So there were bottles of every kind of spirit to be found that day. It was not a luxury, it was a necessity.

Every Packers fan, every football fan or that matter, has seen the image a thousand times. Bart Starr signaling for the ball and taking an ever-so-slight jab step before sliding between Jerry Kramer and Ken Bowman for the winning touchdown. It is an image taught to Packers fans from the time they are old enough to know what a football is.

It has been two generations now since that game was played and perhaps thousands of players have come and gone. Players new to the Packers organization always ask the same question: where did Bart Starr sneak into the end zone in the Ice Bowl? They know the story of the team they're joining, and they know the significance of the team they play for.

Tim Krumrie, who ended up as All-Pro for the Cincinnati Bengals and is perhaps best known for his tackle in 1992 that injured starting quarterback Don Majkowski and led to the emergence of Brett Favre, was born and raised in Wisconsin. He watched Packers games growing up and attended the University of Wisconsin, hoping against hope he'd be drafted by the Packers and play professionally for his beloved team.

Instead, he went to the Bengals but still remembers the opportunities he had to play at Lambeau Field.

"For a Wisconsin kid, you can't imagine when you're playing there in Lambeau Field," he said. "What I remember is the intensity. Oh my God, that's what I remember. You just love the Green Bay Packers and all the wins they've had and all the championships. When you go into the stadium, you learn fast you better watch out. You better be ready to play."

Today, Lambeau Field remains special. It is now more than twice the size of what it was when it first built, seating more than 81,000 fans. It now features restaurants in its atrium and specialty seats line the stadium and a state of the art video board tells fans everything they want, and need, to know.

The latest renovation took place in 2015 and features the "Titletown District" which also includes restaurants and bars. After all, the Green Bay Packers may still hold the quaint titles as the NFL's smallest city, but it is still part of the multibillion-dollar NFL and has to generate income to pay its players to say competitive.

But deep down, Lambeau Field remains what it was always meant to be, a stadium for everyone. And the fans, many of whom weren't even born when the Ice Bowl was played, understand and protect the legacy.

"It's just a special place," Krumrie said.

6

THE GAME

HISTORY AND LEGEND and time and rumor and memory have combined with simple facts to turn the 1967 NFL Championship Game between the Green Bay Packers and the Dallas Cowboys into whatever anyone wants it to be.

Was it a great football? In many ways, yes. Was it a triumph of man over the elements? Sure. Was it some human tragedy in which one team, which was probably better than the other, did not win because the cursed elements conspired against it? If you like. Was it a game of irony that featured a boatload of eventual

Hall of Fame players but decided by journeymen? Certainly. Was it a game that never should been played in the first place? Perhaps.

Maybe that's why the game that came to know as the Ice Bowl continues to resonate over the years. Everyone can take from it what they want.

Perhaps more than anything, though, the game was a human drama that showed an enthralled audience around the country what athletes could do when they needed to do it.

"The elements played a part," said Dallas halfback Dan Reeves, who played such a prominent role in the game. "But there was more to it."

Packers left tackle Bob Skoronski, one of those unsung heroes of the game, recalled that he realized during the game just what they were all involved in.

"For me, it was probably the most concentrated effort I've ever given in a football game," he said. "I thought of all the ways I couldn't let my teammates down. We all knew what was at stake."

In some ways, The Ice Bowl was a play in four acts, each connected with the other but each also a separate drama.

It begins with the realization that winter in Green Bay had hit with a vengeance. That's Act I.

"I remember running to the window of my hotel room and throwing open the drapes and looking outside," Cowboys linebacker Lee Roy Jordan said. "I wanted to see what twenty below looked like."

He saw it and he was speechless, especially given what they had all experienced the day before.

Dallas Cowboys coach Tom Landry watches quarterback Don Meredith warm up in preparation for the NFL Championship Game in January 1967 at the Cotton Bowl. Meredith was one of the first building blocks Landry brought in as he put the new Dallas franchise together. A gritty competitor who played through many injuries, Meredith never could solve the Packers. The loss in Dallas was tough enough on Meredith but the one the following year in Green Bay hurt even more because he was convinced the Cowboys were the better team.

Green Bay's Elijah Pitts picks up yardage in the 1966 NFL Championship Game at the Cotton Bowl. That game, a raucous 34–27 affair, was, in the eyes of many players, a better game than the one played a year later in Green Bay. It certainly helped establish a great rivalry and convince the Cowboys they had what it took to beat the Packers.

For Packers quarterback Bart Starr, the hiring of Vince Lombardi as Green Bay's head coach in 1959 was a career saver. For Lombardi, Starr was the type of quarterback who would run his offense the way Lombardi knew it needed to be run. For Starr, Lombardi allowed him to play to his strengths as a smart, unflappable leader. And in their nine years together, they won five championships. Here, Lombardi congratulates Starr after a first-round playoff win over the Los Angeles Rams in 1967. The Ice Bowl would follow the next week.

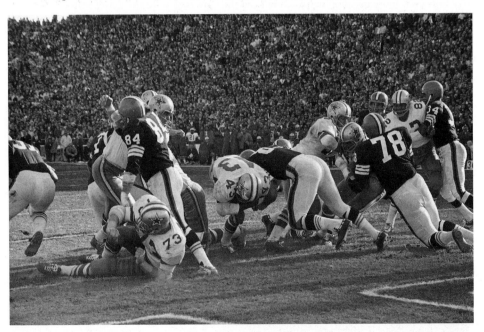

Dallas Cowboys fullback Don Perkins slams into the end zone for a touchdown against the Cleveland Browns in a first-round playoff win in 1967. Perkins, who played for the Cowboys from 1961 to '68, was the team's first great running back, earning six Pro Bowl appearances and rushing for 6,217 yards, which is still third in team history.

Vince Lombardi's pride and joy was a state of the art electrical system he had installed under the Lambeau Field turf that would tame the harsh Wisconsin winters and make the field playable in any weather. He was so proud of it, in fact, he showed it off to the visiting media who had come to town to cover the 1967 title game. What he hadn't counted on was his new system malfunctioning in the intense cold and turning the surface into a virtual skating rink by the end of the game.

A capacity crowd of more than 50,000 fans filed into Lambeau Field in 16 below weather to watch their team. Cowboys scout Gil Brandt recalled looking in the stands a half hour before game time and seeing no one in attendance. But by kickoff, the stands were full. "It was un-believable," he said.

Packers wide receiver Boyd Dowler hauls in his second of two touchdown passes from Bart Starr, this one a 43-yarder over Cowboys defensive back Mel Renfro. Dowler was one of the unsung heroes of the game, catching four passes for 77 yards, including a crucial 13-yard reception on the game's final drive.

Cowboys defensive end George Andrie, with support from teammate Jethro Pugh (75), rumbles into the end zone for a second quarter touchdown that changed the momentum of the Ice Bowl. Willie Townes had forced Bart Starr to fumble and Andrie was there to pick it up and cut the Green Bay lead to 14–7. Green Bay would not mount another offensive drive until the final four desperate minutes of the game.

A key play, and one often overlooked, came in the third quarter when the Cowboys mounted an impressive drive deep into Green Bay territory and seemed ready to take the lead. But on a scramble, quarterback Don Meredith was hit by linebacker Lee Roy Caffey and fumbled. Cornerback Herb Adderley recovered at the Packers' 18-yard line, ending the threat. Caffey made several big plays during the game, but none was bigger than that one.

With Packers safety Tom Brown in futile pursuit, Cowboys flanker Lance Rentzel heads to the end zone after catching Dan Reeves's halfback option pass on the first play of the fourth quarter in the Ice Bowl. That stunning play, and the dominance of the Cowboys' "Doomsday Defense," gave some players on the Dallas sideline the hope that this would be their day. But the Packers' final drive ended those thoughts.

One of the many iconic images of the Ice Bowl. Bart Starr has taken the snap from center Ken Bowman and prepares to squeeze through the hole opened by Bowman and right guard Jerry Kramer that allowed him to score the winning touchdown with 16 seconds to play. To this day, many Cowboys players insist Kramer committed a false start penalty.

Another view of the touchdown from behind the end zone. On the bottom is Starr (15). Notice fullback Chuck Mercein (30) on top of him. Mercein, a relatively unknown player thrown into action due to an injury to starting fullback Jim Grabowski, had already played a superb game and thought he was getting the ball on that play. He was as surprised as everyone else when Starr kept it.

With the final score emblazoned on the scoreboard in the background, Packers fans celebrate the victory over the Cowboys by tearing down the goalposts. Two weeks later, the Packers beat the Oakland Raiders to win Super Bowl II. Only a few weeks after that, Vince Lombardi stepped down as head coach, ending an incredible era in Green Bay.

Packers coach Vince Lombardi congratulates fullback Chuck Mercein after the Ice Bowl victory. Claimed on waivers only weeks earlier after injuries decimated the Packers backfield, Mercein recovered an early fumble and then made several key runs on the final drive that led to Green Bay's win. "He took a chance on me," Mercein said of Lombardi, "and I'll never forget it."

Vince Lombardi is carried off the field by right guard Jerry Kramer after the Packers' 33–14 victory over the Oakland Raiders in Super Bowl II on January 14, 1968. Kramer, and other veterans, had an inkling this was Lombardi's last game as Green Bay's head coach and wanted to send him out with what he craved most—a third straight world championship. Just a few weeks later, Lombardi made the decision official, remaining as general manager but handing over head coaching duties to his longtime defensive coordinator, Phil Bengtson. It was the end of an era.

Vince Lombardi celebrates the Super II victory with two key players from that game—Don Chandler, left, and Bart Starr. Chandler kicked four field goals and Starr was named the game's MVP. But in the minds of many NFL fans, including Packers and Cowboys players, the real league championship had been played two weeks earlier on the frozen field in Green Bay, Wisconsin.

That Saturday, by all accounts and given the realities of playing football in the upper Midwest in late December, was a terrific day to be in Green Bay, Wisconsin.

As the Dallas Cowboys worked out at Lambeau Field the day before the game, the temperatures hovered in the thirties with a blinding blue Arctic sky and no wind. The Cowboys knew all about what it was like to play in Green Bay at this time of year and they knew that this place could provide a home-field advantage like no other.

Teams that played in Green Bay in November and December (there was really no January football back then) knew that the odds were against them because they did not have to deal with that weather on a consistent basis the way Packers players did.

Yes, the weather was cold in Chicago and Detroit and Minnesota that time of year too. But there was something about the Green Bay cold that seeped into the bones and the nervous system and the psyche of any player who wasn't prepared for it.

It was a penetrating cold that sapped your strength and your will. The wind could whip into the Lambeau Field bowl, sometimes off the nearby Fox River and sometimes from the actual bay of Green Bay itself, dropping temperatures ever more.

And if it snowed? Well forget it. All the Packers had to often do was just show up and they already held a two-touchdown lead before the opening kickoff. The mental advantage could never be discounted.

That was evident the week before when the Packers played the Los Angeles Rams in the opening round of the playoffs at the Packers' home away from home, Milwaukee County Stadium.

The temperature that day was a relatively balmy 20 degrees, but the Packers could sense before the game that they already had the advantage.

"The Rams were so freaked out by the cold weather," said Packers safety Doug Hart. "They were saying to each other in warm-ups, 'We're only to be cold for two and a half hours.' That's when I knew we had them."

The Packers didn't even play that well against the powerful Rams, committing four turnovers. But the visitors could nothing with those gifts, and the Packers eventually exerted their will on the way to a 28–7 win.

It had been a long, difficult season for the Packers, perhaps the most trying during the Lombardi era. Injuries to both the offense and the defense had wracked them and only now, as the playoffs began, were the Packers back to anything close to full strength.

And right guard Jerry Kramer could feel something different in his team, something he had never really felt before.

"Coach [Lombardi] had come into the locker room before the Rams game and said in church that morning he had heard about how there are many runners in the race and only one prize," he said. "He told us, 'So let's run the race to win.' It wasn't how he usually talked to us before games. It's as if he'd been driving us and himself all these years and it was time to pull back a little. There was a good feeling, a good atmosphere in the locker room."

That feeling had carried over to the championship game, even as the weather tried to change that dynamic.

For their part, the visiting Cowboys knew they were ready in ways they had not been the year before.

The coaching staff had prepared their team for every eventuality they could run into against the Packers. Several players admitted that the year before they had been starstruck by their first appearance on the championship stage, which played a part in falling behind 14–0 quickly and never quite being able to catch up.

This year would be different. They were smarter, more mature and, most important, while they believed they were the equal of the Packers in 1966, they knew they were the better team this year.

"We did feel like we were a better team from the year before because of the experience from the previous year," said Dan Reeves. "We knew it would be difficult playing them at home but we felt we were the better team. We were very confident."

And there was every reason to think so. The Packers had been banged up all season, and age was catching up to them. Everyone knew it and could see it.

The rugged fullback, Jim Taylor, was gone, signed as a free agent by the New Orleans Saints, who joined the league that season. Paul Hornung had been left unprotected in the expansion draft and he, too, was signed by the Saints. The offensive line was older and battered as was the defensive front and the linebacker corps.

Perhaps most serious were the injuries to steady, stable quarterback Bart Starr. He had missed several games early in the season with injuries ranging from a bad shoulder to bruised ribs to a sprained right thumb.

He returned by midseason but he was not the same player who had been named the MVP in the first Super Bowl.

And while there was still the aura around a Packers team that was trying desperately to win a third straight title, there was also the reality of an aging, injured team that was not what it had been.

"We were the team of the decade," Ken Bowman said. "But I think there was a realism about what we were becoming. We didn't have Jimmy Taylor. We didn't have Paul Hornung. We didn't have the stars of the early Packers. We had kind of a make-shift team. But we were still the champions until somebody beat us when it mattered."

And Bowman knew, as did every other Packers player, that Lombardi was driven, perhaps almost to mania, to take this team to a third straight championship. Indeed, Lombardi, who was already starting to develop the health issues that in a little more than three years would kill him, drove himself that season almost as hard as he drove his team.

"I'd play bridge on the west side of Green Bay every week and I'd drive by Lambeau Field late at night I'd see lights flickering in the window and know what Lombardi was doing," Bowman recalled. "There was somebody running that projector and there was only one guy who would be doing that."

Still, the Cowboys rolled into town a confident team. Weather, experience, circumstances, none of that really mattered because deep down they believed this was the year the Packers dynasty ended. And they were the ones to end it.

Reeves remembered the team going through a Saturday work-out at Lambeau Field and everyone marveled at the relatively quiet conditions. So now, they began to think, even the weather would cooperate.

"We worked out the day before and the forecast for the next day was supposed to be basically what we worked out in," he said. "The sun was shining. It was cold but there was no wind and there was sunshine. It was really a pretty nice day. The field was in great shape. And the weather we worked out in was forecast for the next day."

"I would have loved to have played if it had been the way it was the day before," said Lee Roy Jordan.

But overnight, the vagaries of the Wisconsin winter were unleashed. An arctic front whipped in from the north, dragging in frigid temperatures and, worse, wind.

Had players on both teams expected what was to come, they might have been mentally prepared for what awaited them. But neither team knew what was to come, and the results the next morning were met with a mixture of disbelief, bemusement, and concern.

The Cowboys, who were staying in Appleton thirty miles away, got their wakeup calls, and none could believe what they heard.

Jordan remembers it as though it were yesterday.

"Good morning!" the caller said. "It's 7:30 and it's sixteen below outside."

Wide receiver Lance Rentzel thought it was joke. Fellow wide receiver Bob Hayes couldn't believe it.

It wasn't much better from the Packers side.

"Some fellas couldn't get their cars started," Bowman said. "One guy, I heard, came in on a snowmobile [actually it was five of them]. My car was in an underground garage so I didn't have any problems. But I got a sense that those from Dallas didn't want to be here. They were a fair-weather team. They were a very good team, but they weren't used to something like this. Of course, neither was I. But Dallas is a whole lot nicer in the winter than Green Bay."

Fullback Chuck Mercein, who had been added to the Packers roster only weeks earlier as insurance for gimpy starter Jim Grabowski, was roused awake by his clock radio. He still remembers the words he heard that even today make him shiver.

"It said, 'It's thirteen below zero," he recalled. "I didn't think I'd heard it right. I'd never been in anything like that before."

It was so unfathomable that many players, especially on the Cowboys side, figured NFL commissioner Pete Rozelle would postpone the game because no one could play effectively in that kind of weather and, certainly, fans (even in Wisconsin) would not venture out into such conditions.

"Yeah, we were kind of hoping the commissioner would call it off,' Jordan recalled with a laugh. "But he wasn't even there. He was at the game in Oakland [the AFL Championship Game to be played later in the day]. He made the call that it would go on."

Bowman, who had grown up in Illinois and played football at the University of Wisconsin and then with the Packers, never had a doubt it would be played.

"It was a championship game," Bowman said simply. "Of course we were going to play. You don't postpone championship games."

And so, as much mentally as physically, both teams prepared to play a game in conditions none of them had ever seen before.

But the temperature proved to be only part of the problem. The real issue, as the players soon learned, would involve the field itself. After all, there were ways to, in theory at least, keep relatively warm. But if there was a problem with the field, then both teams would be relegated to earliest days of pro football, when running the ball was the only option.

And there was indeed a problem with the field.

As with just about everything involved with the game, stories emerged as to just what happened to the so-called frozen tundra of Lambeau Field.

Chuck Lane, the Packers director of public relations at the time, had been headed out to check the field when several assistant coaches came up to him with the bad news. The field was frozen. Not a little frozen either; rock-solid frozen.

Lane had the unenviable task of delivering the news to Lombardi, who was on his way to check the field himself.

Told it was for all intents and purposes an ice rink, Lombardi was at first incredulous and then furious. It wasn't supposed to be that way.

Earlier in the spring, Lombardi had spent $80,000 to have a new electric blanket installed under the turf to ward off the ravages of a Wisconsin winter, and Packers beat writers were amused by the time and attention Lombardi had spent on his pride and joy.

It was state of the art technology for the late 1960s and featured electric coils laid out in a grid that spanned the length of the field. The coils were buried six inches below the surface with another six inches of gravel below that and a drainage system under that. It was, perhaps, the first real effort by man to battle the effects of nature.

And it was all coordinated from a tiny control room under the stands of Lambeau Field.

Lombardi had been so proud of the project that the day before the championship game, he showed it off to the national media who had come to cover the game. He tried to converse like an expert on what the coils would do but most of the bemused writers knew he was simply a football coach from New Jersey trying his best to explain something he didn't really understand.

But it was working, and that's really all Lombardi cared about. In its first real test, Lambeau Field was uncovered Saturday to allow the Cowboys to practice and the turf was in good shape. Even Tom Landry said the field was in "excellent" shape if a little damp. Lombardi looked on from afar and beamed.

But overnight, the coil system had malfunctioned, and the moisture that was being drawn out of the covered field was now freezing on the surface. And on Sunday as the field was uncovered for the game, the soft, damp turf of the day before was now rock hard. And it would only get worse as the entire field froze by the second half.

Rumors swirled for years that Lombardi had intentionally turned off the heating system as a way to slow down the Cowboys. But observers at the time said from Lombardi's reaction to the faulty electrical system, there was no way he planned it. After all, what slowed down the Cowboys also slowed down the Packers.

In the final analysis, most of the players said in fact it wasn't the cold that was the biggest problem (thought it was big enough), it was the condition of the field. No one could gain any traction and players, both on offense and defense, who were used to running at full speed to make a play were now tip-toeing along the turf.

The Cowboys especially felt impacted. They possessed a fast, swarming defense and an offense predicated on big plays (and averaged 335 yards per game), especially to their fleet wideouts Bob Hayes and Lance Rentzel.

And well before the game even started, Hayes had already all but checked out mentally and physically from the festivities

A Florida native who had played his college ball at Florida A&M and was considered the fastest human alive after winning the 100-meter dash in the 1964 Summer Olympics, he had never experienced such cold in his life.

"Hayes just didn't want to be there," Lee Roy Jordan said with a laugh. "He would have wanted to be anywhere else but there. It was something he just couldn't overcome mentally. I keep thinking that if we'd had a little bit better conditions, we had a chance to win the game. Our offense didn't produce as many points as we usually did because of it. The weather eliminated a lot of our passing game. I would have loved for the weather to have been the way it was the day before. That was perfect."

Dan Reeves, who played his college ball at South Carolina, still remembers how cold it was.

"It's been gone over so many times but I'll never forget," Reeves said. "I know that prior to the game, we went out to see what the conditions were and I caught a few passes. It was like catching a brick. I held for extra points and it was the same. It was awful. There were people who worked in the dressing room and they to put Saran Wrap around our feet. But the Saran Wrap would break when you made a cut and then you'd really feel the cold. It was something I'd never experienced before. You just never thought it could get that cold."

And while it's thought the Packers took the weather in stride, it really was no better for them.

In fact, unlike Bowman, who never doubted that the game would be played, Packers safety Willie Wood was certain the NFL, in its infinite wisdom and as a matter of common sense, would postpone it.

"It's just too damn cold," he told fellow defensive back Bob Jeter. "They're not going to play in this."

But that proved wishful thinking when Lombardi emerged from his office to declare the game was on and everyone should get ready.

Both Landry and Lombardi were from the oldest of old schools, which meant they didn't want offensive players who handled the ball to wear gloves for fear of fumbling. The same went with their defensive players, who used their hands to fend off blocks and to tackle. With gloves, they wouldn't have the proper grip.

But Packers linebacker Dave Robinson had a solution for that and asked for a pair of brown gloves. With his brown skin, he determined no one would ever know the difference.

"The elements played such a part," Reeves recalled. "You couldn't even stand up. The elements were difficult to handle. We just didn't have all the things then that they do now to handle the cold. Coach Landry wouldn't let you wear gloves if you handled the ball. So you shoved your hands down your pants and when came off the field, you got in front of the heater."

It was finally time to play the game. The pregame questions and concerns no longer mattered. The field was freezing up, but at least both teams would have to deal with it. No one was going to call it off and it was time for Act II of the play. Let's call it Instant Replay.

"At kickoff, the footing was tolerable," Starr said. "I don't think any of us knew how bad it would get as the game went on."

The Cowboys had always believed if they hadn't struggled so badly at the start of the championship game in 1966 that they would have won. They knew they needed a better start this time around.

They didn't get it. Though they got the ball first and got a quick first down on a pass from Don Meredith to Bob Hayes, the drive stalled and the Packers also gained a valuable key to the rest of the game.

They saw that on plays where Hayes was not involved, he would stand at the line of scrimmage with his hands jammed deep down the front of his pants. When he was the primary receiver, the hands would be out. After that first catch for 10 yards, Hayes was a non-factor, catching two more passes for just six yards.

The Packers got the ball on their own 18-yard line after a punt and on the first play, a nice five-yard run by Donny Anderson, he fumbled. A disastrous early turnover was avoided when Chuck Mercein, Green Bay's new fullback, fell on it.

It was just the first of several big plays the unknown and unheralded Mercein would make that day.

In truth, that Mercein was even on the field as a member of the Packers was a combination of serendipity and good, old-fashioned luck. Originally a third-round draft pick of the New York Giants in 1965, he thought he'd get the opportunity to be New York's new fullback. But in the first round of the same draft, the Giants also selected Tucker Frederickson, the 1964 Heisman Trophy runner-up.

At that stage, Mercein knew his options were limited. It also led to a standoff with head coach Allie Sherman.

"Allie and I just got off on the wrong foot," Mercein said. "I was disappointed and frustrated."

Mercein eventually gained his release early in the 1967 and had planned to sign with the Washington Redskins when Lombardi contacted him.

"I was going to sign with the Redskins on Monday and Sunday night the Packers called," he said. "Coach Lombardi asked if I wanted to play for the Packers and I said, 'Sure.' He took a chance on me. He resurrected a career that had gone off the rails in New York."

Mercein was brought in for insurance after injuries to running backs Elijah Pitts and Jim Grabowksi. It had been hoped that Grabowski, who had been dealing a knee injury for several weeks, would be healthy enough to play that day. But during pregame warm-ups, the fullback went out on a simple pattern and reinjured his knee, which put him out for the game.

Mercein slid up in the rotation and with that fumble recovery had already made his presence felt.

And, not unlike the championship game the year before, Lombardi had found a way to attack Landry's flex defense. Green Bay's seasoned, rugged offensive line was pushing the defensive linemen back and into the "bubble" that was created as part of Dallas's attacking defense.

With Anderson running just enough to keep the defense off balance and thanks to two Cowboys penalties and Starr completing four of five passes for 57 yards, including an 8-yard touchdown strike to Boyd Dowler, the Packers had taken the early lead with a systematic 14-play, 82-yard drive.

It was Green Bay Packers football at its most elemental and dangerous.

As the second quarter opened, the Packers started a drive on their own 35. And Lombardi, who for years had been considered a predictable coach who did only a few things but did them all well, again came up with a wrinkle.

He replaced Anderson and Mercein with speedy halfback Travis Williams, who had made a name for himself that season by returning four kickoffs for touchdowns. But now he was in the backfield and carried three straight times for 22 yards.

Facing third down and a yard from the Dallas 43, Starr again found Dowler for the touchdown and a 14–0 lead.

It was 1966 all over again. The Packers, though beaten up and aging, had shown the challengers what it took to be champions.

The Cowboys, who had come to Green Bay convinced, at least in the words of fullback Don Perkins, that they'd "beat the stuffing out of the Packers" were in the same position they were a year earlier. And conditions were far worse.

It was getting colder and the field was getting icier.

Referee Norm Schachter had seen umpire Joe Connell lose half of his lower lip when his metal whistle had stuck to the skin. As well, the wooden balls in the whistles were frozen in place and from early in the game, it was determined no whistles would be used. When a play was over, the officials gave verbal commands.

The University of Wisconsin-LaCrosse marching band, which was supposed to play at halftime, figured out in the first half that would not happen since most of the instruments had already frozen.

Later in the game, Reeves was getting up after a play and collided with Packers tackle Ron Kostelnik.

"It was so cold my facemask busted and I had my tooth come up through my upper lip," he said. "It didn't even bleed."

And the sideline heaters that both teams counted on for some semblance of warmth began to malfunction and those that did work sent warm air into the ground, creating a muddy mess.

But through all of this, the game was about to enter Act III, the Dallas Domination.

A two-touchdown lead in these conditions should have been more than enough, especially for these Packers. But in the final four minutes of the first half, it was the Packers who were suddenly impacted by the weather.

The Cowboys defense, especially the fast and physical front four, had already been harassing Starr for most of the half. But on first down and 15 from his own 26, Starr dropped back to pass only to see what amounts to the entire Dallas front four of George Andrie, Willie Townes, Jethro Pugh, and the ubiquitous Bob Lilly coming after him.

The usually unflappable Starr then made a major gaffe, scrambling backward toward his own goal line. He was hit by Townes and fumbled at his own 7. Andrie picked up the ball and rumbled into the end zone for the touchdown.

Just like that, the Packers' safe two-touchdown lead was cut in half.

But it wasn't over. Two minutes later, the usually surehanded punt returner Willie Wood, who admitted afterward he could not even feel his hands, fumbled a fair catch attempt. The ball was recovered by Dallas's Frank Clarke at the Green Bay 17. Four plays later, Danny Villanueva kicked a 21-yard field goal.

Two key mistakes by Packers who rarely made any had given new life to a Cowboys team that was probably close to giving up when it had fallen behind by two touchdowns.

Now, it was a game.

In later years, Starr talked about how many people still underrated the Cowboys.

"They were talented, physical, and well-prepared," Starr said. "We had more experience, but they had earned the right to be there."

In the locker room at halftime, the Cowboys were beyond encouraged. They had absorbed the best of what the Packers had to offer and were still standing. Indeed, they knew the momentum had changed and if they could continue their defensive domination, the offense would be able to do just enough to take control. It was there for the taking.

In the Packers locker room, a sense of concern hung over everything like a cloud. They were cold and angry and discouraged and they were beginning to feel like the team most people thought had seen their best days.

The Cowboys defense had clearly taken over and the Green Bay offense was skidding and sliding and going nowhere fast. Since the second touchdown pass to Dowler early in the second quarter, the Packers, in 13 offensive plays, had lost yardage or gained nothing on five of them.

As almost a cruel reminder of what had been, Lombardi had asked Paul Hornung to join him on the sideline for the game.

Hornung had been perhaps Lombardi's all-time favorite player, someone he called "like a son to me."

Lombardi had rejuvenated Hornung's career in 1959, identifying him as the perfect halfback in his new offense. Hornung would go on to earn the 1961 league MVP award and become the symbol of a dominant Packers running game.

Yes, he had disappointed the "Old Man" with his year-long NFL suspension in 1963. The two could collide daily on any issue under the sun but in the end they respected and loved each other. Lombardi even famously called President John Kennedy in 1961 to spring Hornung free from his military obligation that would have landed at the same time as the championship game against the New York Giants. Kennedy made the call and Hornung scored a touchdown and kicked three goals and four extra points in a 37–0 Packers win.

But injuries caught up with Hornung in 1966 and in 1967, he was made available for the New Orleans Saints expansion draft. It was a move Hornung requested, mostly because he loved New Orleans and already had hammered out a new radio deal with a station down there. Hornung knew his playing days were done and he never played a down for the Saints.

But when it came time for the Packers to play in the '67 title game, Lombardi requested Hornung join him in the sidelines. He agreed but that, of course, was before Hornung knew what the weather would be.

Hornung recalled that day:

"I was standing next to Lombardi nearly the entire game and he did the same thing, asking me if I saw any plays I liked to let him know. I never did because you really didn't tell Lombardi anything. At the time, I said, 'No sir, I don't." I wasn't going to tell him anything because I thought he might run the damn thing."

Hornung had also been scheduled to be interviewed by Pat Summerall at halftime for CBS-TV. But Hornung said was so cold he could not open his mouth to talk. And talking was never a problem for Paul Hornung. So the interview was cancelled.

"I don't care what they say about games today," Hornung said. "I'm not sure it will ever be colder that it was that day. That game should have been postponed. I have no idea why it wasn't."

Neither team scored in the third quarter. In fact, the only winner was the weather, which, as the sun dipped below the Lambeau Field rim, saw the temperature continue to plummet. By that stage, the entire playing surface was ice.

Players from both teams felt a particular tingling and then a numbness on their extremities that were the early stages of frostbite. It seemed that the next score, if there was one, would probably determine the winner.

And that appeared more and more likely to be the Cowboys, who had completely taken over the momentum.

In their only real drive of the game, the Cowboys moved from their own 11 to the Packers 18 in eight plays. Meredith completed three of four passes for 32 yards and Reeves took over the bulk of the running, gaining 31 yards on three carries.

But linebacker Lee Roy Caffey, another one of the unheralded players who rose up for the Packers that day, was key in keeping the Cowboys off the scoreboard.

First, he dropped Reeves for a four-yard loss back to the Packers 22 on first down. After a Meredith incompletion on second down, the Cowboys quarterback dropped back to throw again. Pressured by the Green Bay defense, he started running and was hit by Caffey, forcing a fumble that was recovered by Green Bay's Herb Adderley at the Packers 13.

Caffey was another of those players who had come to Green Bay with a little baggage and who flourished in the system.

Drafted originally in the seventh round by the Philadelphia Eagles in 1963, the Texas native was dealt to the Packers in May 1964 as part of the infamous Jim Ringo trade. Lombardi knew he had potential, but he also had a reputation for being lazy and not practicing hard. And practicing hard was a requirement in the Lombardi regime.

Nicknamed the "big turkey" by Lombardi, he was able to get the best out of the linebacker and, paired with Ray Nitschke and Dave Robinson, they formed perhaps the finest linebacking crew in team history.

In the Ice Bowl, those two plays were dramatic, and on top of that, he added two more tackles for losses at a time when the Packers defense was struggling.

Caffey was traded to the Cowboys in 1970 and enjoyed a few more years in the league. But he never forgot his years in Green Bay, especially with Lombardi.

Kramer, whose love of Lombardi spanned the decades, had never thought Caffey and Lombardi got along. But his view on that changed during a team reunion in 1985, the fifteen-year anniversary of Lombardi's death.

"Just about every guy from Super Bowl I was at a crossroads in his life," Kramer recalled. "For example, Lee Roy Caffey had a bank charter down in Texas that he tried to get four of five different times. But they'd turned him down every time. Lee Roy's partners were getting discouraged and wanted to quit and he said, 'You can quit, but I can't. If Lombardi found out, he'd kill me.' When I saw the depth of that impact, it made me feel like there was still something to say. That's what really got me. I mean, Lombardi had been dead for fifteen years. I didn't expect that."

Caffey's play in that game is still pointed to by many Packers as the key to Green Bay's win.

Dallas's next possession started at the Green Bay 48 but only reached the Packers 39. Villanueva's 47-yard field goal attempt never had a chance.

The Packers had dodged two bullets, but with an offense that was going nowhere, it only seemed a matter of time before the Cowboys finally broke through.

That opportunity finally arrived on the first play of the fourth quarter. The Cowboys had kept the play called "Fire Pitch" available all day, waiting for the right situation to run it. Now, with the ball sitting at the 50-yard line and conditions continuing to deteriorate, the Cowboys looked at each other in the huddle.

Depending on who you talk to, it was either wide receiver Lance Rentzel, halfback Dan Reeves, or quarterback Don Meredith who called the play.

It was a halfback option pass that every team has in their arsenal. But the Cowboys used it more than most teams, mostly because they had a halfback in Reeves who had been a quarterback in college. In his three seasons with the Cowboys, Reeves had thrown that pass 15 times and completed eight for two touchdowns.

And Reeves was ready.

"I spent time before that play with my hands jammed down my pants to keep them warm," he said.

On the snap, Reeves pitched the ball to Reeves who ran to the left. In the past, they had always run the play to the right since Reeves was right-handed and it made the throw easier. But the Cowboys also realized that the Packers knew that.

Seeing Reeves running left, cornerbacks Bob Jeter and Willie Wood came up to stop him. That pursuit allowed Rentzel to slip behind the secondary, and free safety Tom Brown was too far away to make up the distance.

Jeter said later, "I was slow mentally on that play. I saw Reeves cock his arm. I tried to get back, but when the ball was in the air, I knew it was gone."

Rentzel's concern was being able to hang onto the ball as it cut through the frozen air.

"It was a marvelous feeling," he said afterward.

The Cowboys had finally struck, taking a 17–14 lead and were poised to take their first NFL title.

After an exchange of punts, Green Bay drove to the Dallas 33, but Don Chandler came up short on a game-tying field goal attempt.

Taking over at their 20 with a little more than nine minutes to play, the Cowboys knew a long drive or, better yet, another score could end any doubt. And Dallas did indeed put together a nice march, converting two huge third downs including a dramatic 16-yard completion to Clarke at the Dallas 47 on 3rd and 10.

But the Cowboys could do nothing after that, and Willie Wood took the ensuing punt nine yards from the Packers 23 to the 32.

Call Act IV "The Drive." Everyone else does.

Perhaps no 12 plays in the history of professional football have been analyzed and scrutinized the way these have. And why not?

There was no evidence that the Packers could do this. Since early in the second quarter when they scored their last touchdown, the Packers had 10 possessions consisting of 31 plays. They had gained minus nine yards and Bart Starr had been hammered. Five of his passes had been batted down, and he had been sacked eight times.

Now, with 4:54 left to play and the ball sitting on their own 32-yard line, they would have to find an inner strength and perseverance no one was sure was there anymore.

Lombardi and Starr had decided on the sideline not to try for a quick score, but to work the ball down the field and score. That's what the Packers had always done, and it's what they did now. They would succeed or fail playing the only way they knew how.

In the huddle, Starr was calm.

"I looked into the eyes of my teammates and I knew instantly that nothing needed to be said," Starr said. "They knew the importance."

"I don't think anybody said a whole lot," center Ken Bowman said. "I think we all knew this was the last time we'd see the ball and we thought we have to get it down there so Chandler can kick a danged field goal and send it to overtime."

"I looked into everyone's eyes," said guard Jerry Kramer. "There was awareness, understanding, determination. Everybody knew what we had to do."

After looking at everyone in the huddle, Starr finally said the only thing that needed to be said: "OK, this is it. Let's get it done."

Not every Packers player, however, held that kind of steely resolve that all would be well.

"I hate to say it, but I'd lost faith in the offense," linebacker Dave Robinson said years later. "They hadn't done a thing. The Cowboys had shut them down completely."

And the Packers were set to embark on perhaps the greatest drive in NFL history. Make no mistake, though, the drive does not happen without Starr, who had been battered all day by the Cowboys.

"Starr had a very commanding presence in the huddle," Mercein said. "We felt calm, poised and confident and that came from Bart. He was in charge of that huddle."

But on the other sideline, the Cowboys were allowing themselves to think that, perhaps, this was indeed their day.

"We really thought we were going to win the game," Ralph Neely said.

The key for the Packers on that last drive was to mount something, anything, positive. It started on the first play when Starr, taking advantage of the Cowboys linebackers' penchant for dropping deep to help with coverage of the wide receivers, hit Donny Anderson for a 6-yard gain in the right flat. It wasn't much, but it was a start.

The next play saw Mercein run right for seven yards and stumble out of bounds for a first down at the Green Bay 45. It was the first time in seemingly ages that the Packers had put together back-to-back positive plays.

The momentum was building.

On first down, Starr found Dowler over the middle for a 13-yard gain to the Cowboys 42. What's forgotten by many people is that not only was Dowler forearmed in the helmet by linebacker Dave Edwards as he made the catch, his head bounced off the frozen ground. And yet he held onto the ball.

"Boyd Dowler was so underrated," Bowman said.

But any momentum seemed to end immediately when Cowboys defensive end Willie Townes dropped Anderson for a 9-yard loss. But Starr rebounded and found Anderson at the 50, and the halfback eluded linebacker Chuck Howley for another 11 yards to the Dallas 39.

Another pass to Anderson put the ball down to the Dallas 30 and gave the Packers a first down. But now time was becoming an issue. The drive had been Green Bay's best of the day, but there was now just 1:35 left to play.

Mercein followed with another crucial play, making a difficult catch of a Starr pass in the left flat and managing to keep his footing and run 19 yards to the Cowboys 11. Now a tying field goal was at least a possibility though in the gathering gloom, and with the temperature continuing to drop on a completely iced field, even that was no certainty.

Next came the play that set up the final drama. Called "Brown Right, 65-Give," it took advantage of the quickness and intelligence of Cowboys tackle Bob Lilly.

Years later, Bart Starr explained the play as only someone who knew the Packers offense so well and was so meticulous could explain it.

"We waited to run that play until it was perfect for that drive," he said. "I handed the ball to Chuck Mercein on what was called an 'influence' play. If you were looking at the back of our offensive line, our left guard [Gale Gillingham] pulled to the right.

Bob Lilly was opposite him and charging at an angle almost parallel to the line, which meant we could not block him cleanly. We decided to use Lilly's tremendous quickness and anticipation to our advantage. We pulled our guard to the right, hoping that Lilly would try to beat him to the point of attack. This would take Lilly out of the play, which was going to be run to the spot where he originally lined up. This was a risky call, but I believed the time had come to try it, as the adrenaline was running full tilt and Lilly would likely try to make a decisive play for their defense, which he had done so many times.

"There was also a second aspect this play, without which we could not have succeeded. If Lilly took himself out of the intended hole, we knew that the Cowboys' defensive end, George Andrie, would cover the area unless our left tackle, Bob Skoronski, could cut him off."

In the huddle, Starr asked the veteran tackle if he could get over and do the job.

Skoronski said simply, "Call it."

"That's all I needed to hear," Starr recalled.

Starr continued recapping the play call, which he said was the "the most memorable play I ever called."

"The play was a huge success, the highlight of the drive," he said. "Mercein gained eight crucial yards, and if the field had been in better shape, he might have scored. That play perfectly illustrated how important it was for every player to execute his block, because if Skoronski had failed to cut off Andrie, we would have achieved only a one- or two-yard gain. In my opinion, Skoronski should be in the Hall of Fame. He was an outstanding offensive tackle. Had he not been overshadowed by his teammate, Forrest Gregg, one of the best tackles to ever play the game, he would already be in Canton."

Bowman, too, remembers how during meetings that week, the offensive thought there was a way to use Lilly's strength against him

"We were the team of the Green Bay Packers sweep," Bowman said. "Lilly was a jackrabbit and he could run it down from behind. So when Lilly started to follow 'Gilly' that was a big hole. I think Lilly expected the sweep."

The play worked perfectly and Mercein slashed his way for eight yards to the Cowboys 3.

"You could smell a rat," Lilly recalled years later. "But the Packers didn't give away many rats. The Packers just didn't give things away."

He recalled how Andrie knew his responsibility and knew what was coming but as he moved down the line to fill the hole, he slipped on the icy field.

"And that was that," Lilly said simply.

But there was more work to do, and it would prove to be the most difficult, and memorable.

Anderson followed with a two-yard run that put the ball on the Cowboys 1.

Today, there are few football fans who can't re-create what happened in those final pulsating seconds when chances were taken, plays were made and history written.

And yet, as remarkable as that drive had been to that stage, the weather once again figured to win in the end.

The field was icy, and no one could gain any traction.

On his second down run, Anderson was stopped short of the goal line and on third down, he barely kept his footing as he got the handoff from Starr. But look closely at the play and you'll see that not only did Anderson hang onto the ball, he found a hole, stretched out, and appeared to score.

Lee Roy Jordan laughs at the memory today.

"Donny and I are members of the same golf club and every time I see him he still tells me that," Jordan said. "He says he scored before Bart ever did. He wants me to look at film of the Ice Bowl and I'd see it. But I won't watch it. Maybe he did score."

Several Cowboys as well are convinced that not only did Anderson score, but he fumbled as he stretched out and Dallas had recovered.

But neither of those circumstances was even considered in the tumult of the moment. Instead, Starr frantically called his team's final timeout.

"I asked the linemen if they could get their footing for one more wedge play, and they all said yes," Starr recalled.

So during Green Bay's final timeout, Starr trotted to the sideline to discuss what to do next. There was no talk of a field goal. Starr said he could get the traction needed to slip into the end zone.

Every Packers fan now knows that Lombardi looked at his veteran quarterback and said, "Well run it and let's get the hell out of here."

He would call the play "31 Wedge," a play that with the personnel on the field would have called for Starr to hand the ball to Mercein.

But Starr already knew what he was going to do. Even though the Packers had not run a quarterback sneak all season and certainly did not have one set up for that goal line situation, that would be the decision. Difficult times, after all, sometimes call for outrageous decisions.

Told by an assistant coach if the play didn't work, there would be no time to set up a field goal, Lombardi just shook his head.

"We won't need it," he said.

Bowman heard the call and expected Mercein to leap in to the end zone and not Starr to squeeze in. But his job was the same either way.

"I came off the ball and I went low on [tackle] Jethro Pugh," he said. "They were a damn tough team to move off the line. I snapped it and was surprised how high Jethro was. I got into his rib cage and I shoved him backwards and then I see Bart diving into the end zone. I drove Jethro back maybe two yards but that was enough."

Bowman's block, along with the block of right guard Jerry Kramer, cleared the smallest of holes for Starr to sneak through.

Mercein, expecting the ball, was shocked when it didn't come his way but he can be seen diving over Starr, his arms outstretched not, as he has said time and again, to aid Starr into the end zone (which would have been a penalty) but to show officials that he was not helping him.

Kramer remembers looking over at Starr while they were both still lying on the ground and thinking how satisfying it was.

"It was quite a feeling of relief," Kramer said.

There wasn't much celebrating on the Packers sideline after the touchdown. Everyone was too exhausted and frozen and ready for the very long day to be over.

But defensive tackle Henry Jordan did tap defensive coordinator Phil Bengtson on the shoulder and smiled.

"Another day, another dollar, right coach?" he said.

For many players, the significance of the game would not sink in for days. For others, it would take weeks and months and, in some cases, years.

Cowboys linebacker Lee Roy Jordan still reflects on it.

"Anytime you lose, you analyze and it can be a good thing for you," he said. "We took our losses and turned them around. We had to work at it for a long time to get it right before we won a Super Bowl. But we worked at it and finally did it. Those losses to the Packers, especially in the Ice Bowl, were great lessons for us. They found a way to win."

Even the Packers weren't quite sure how they'd done it, but they had. And though it was barely over, the game had already passed into something approaching legend. Of course, no one on either team knew it at the time and didn't really care.

They had survived what many said was their toughest day ever on the football field. And on this day and in those circumstances, survival was good enough.

7

THE AFTERMATH

AND THEN IT was over.

After everything both teams, coaching staffs and, yes, the fans who had braved the ordeal had gone through the previous three hours, it was over.

The Packers, by virtue of one of the most amazing four-minute drives in NFL history, had overcome the icy field, the frozen temperatures, the frostbite, the pain, the uncertainty, and the belief of many football fans that they simply didn't have enough left to win.

The Cowboys had done very much the same thing. Their aptly named "Doomsday Defense" had played brilliantly most of the day until the time it counted the most. They had faced down the team they admired and hated the most, the team they had quietly mocked as over the hill, in the worst conditions possible and nearly won.

The final score lingered and twinkled on the Lambeau Field scoreboard long after the game was over, almost as if the numbers needed to remain visible to make sure they were real.

21–17.

The Packers had shown, perhaps for the last time during this remarkable run, that when it mattered most, they could still get the job done.

"Just watch that final drive," guard Jerry Kramer said. "It personifies the Green Bay Packers of that era."

And as the two teams staggered into their warm locker rooms afterward, they knew in ways they could not yet enunciate that they had taken part in something truly special.

In 1967, NFL championship games were not yet the overwhelming media sensation they would become as the years went by. Still, newspaper and radio reporters waited as did the CBS-TV cameras, all of whom wanted to some context to what they'd just witnessed.

But, not surprisingly, the two locker rooms were contrasts in emotions. Lombardi thundered for the media to "get the hell out" of his locker room so he could have a chance to talk privately with his battered warriors.

In the Dallas locker room, where there were no TV cameras (in those days TV did not interview losing players), Tom Landry holed up in a small office in the impossibly small locker room trying to compose himself. When he finally did, he marched past the reporters to talk individually to his players who had left so much on the frozen field.

"Tough loss," Landry said grimly.

"I guess we just can't win the big one," Cowboys quarterback Don Meredith said bitterly, thinking back to the loss the previous year and the mistakes made late in this one.

The game was there to be won. And then it wasn't and for Meredith, a deeper and more emotional man than he ever let on to the public, would carry both of those losses with him until his death in 2010 at the age of seventy-two.

But he also expounded on how proud he was of his teammates and how everyone, every single player, had expended everything.

And he cried.

Perhaps that was prevalent emotion after it was over.

Relief. Anger. Satisfaction.

And tears.

Packers left guard Fuzzy Thurston, a mainstay on five championship teams but who had lost his starting job that season to the younger Gale Gillingham, wept afterward.

"This was the toughest," he said. "But it was also the most satisfying."

"This game was our mark of distinction," said left tackle Bob Skoronski.

Dan Reeves, whose halfback option touchdown pass on the first play of the fourth could have replaced Starr's sneak as one of NFL's most iconic plays, still thinks about it.

"It was such a disappointment," he said. "To come that close and lose it in last sixteen seconds of the game like that, that's a tough loss. That's about as tough as it gets. You have to give them credit for driving the length of the field and they had some unbelievable plays. Mercein running that sucker play, that was just incredible. And that last play was a huge gamble. We thought it was a going to be a play action pass and if it didn't work they'd still have a chance to kick a field goal."

"All the world loves a gambler," Lombardi triumphantly said to the TV cameras afterward. "Except when he loses."

But the braggadocio he showed to the world belied the emotion he had only minutes earlier when he'd been unable to complete his speech to his team afterward. He tried to tell them how proud he was of them for an effort few figured these Packers still had.

He wanted to tell them how special they were and how they had done something no other team had ever done. And they had done it in circumstances that would have crushed others.

But the words stuck in his throat. And the players all knew it.

Bowman was one of the youngsters, a player who had spent his offseason studying to be a lawyer and who could not understand the hold Lombardi had over the veteran players. But at that moment, he knew.

"I was fortunate to have played for him," he said simply.

For Bart Starr, an interminable season of injury and anguish had continued that day as he was punished and bludgeoned by the Cowboys' remarkable defense.

He was in agony after the game but still managed a smile.

Asked what would have happened if the sneak had failed, Starr just shook his head.

"I don't want to think about that," he said, the smile disappearing from his face.

Lombardi met with the media and spoke about what a gamble it truly was for Starr to try the quarterback sneak on the final play. Starr hated quarterback sneaks and hadn't even attempted one in three years. But both Lombardi and Star knew that was the best play under the circumstances.

What if it had failed, Lombardi was asked, and Jethro Pugh had simply sat on Starr short of the goal line until the clock ran out. It would not have been unlike seven years earlier when, in the championship game against the Philadelphia Eagles, linebacker Chuck Bednarik had stopped Jim Taylor short of the goal line and wouldn't let him up until the game was over.

"Game's over," Bednarik growled. "Now you can get up."

Lombardi smiled at the question and, perhaps, at that memory.

"Yeah, it was a gamble," he said.

He was animated and quotable and as relaxed as many observers had seen him in ages. The "Old Man" was reveling in a win that meant the world to him.

Lombardi cracked that going for the touchdown was, in part, dictated by the weather.

"I didn't figure those fans in the stands wanted to sit through a sudden death [overtime]," he said. "You can't say I'm without compassion, although I've been accused of it."

Then he motioned to the locker room.

"The story's out there, not here."

Indeed it was.

Bowman and linebacker Ray Nitschke were sitting at their lockers with their feet in cold water, which at the time was deemed the best way to deal with frostbite.

"I remember TV people set up a portable stage and they were calling for Kramer to come up and talk about the block," Bowman said. "And as he walked by my locker, I said, 'Don't forget to tell them it was a double team.' He said, 'You're just young kid. You'll have plenty of time to make another block like that. I'm old. This is for me. I figured he was right. I was twenty-four years old. But there was never another block like that."

Players were asked to talk about the game and what they had accomplished, and many still couldn't put it into words.

There were several players who had contributed so much to the game. Bart Starr and Jerry Kramer and Chuck Mercein and Lee Roy Caffey and Dan Reeves and Jethro Pugh and Bob Lilly and Don Meredith had all made huge plays. But there were also players who had been lost in the tide of history.

One was Boyd Dowler, the veteran receiver whose two receptions on the Packers' first two possessions gave Green Bay a 14–0 lead that would send an early message.

In a 2015 interview with the *Milwaukee Journal Sentinel*'s Michael Cohen, Dowler recalled that second TD reception of the game remains perhaps the most memorable of a career that spanned 12 seasons from 1959 to 1971 with the first 11 in Green Bay.

"I caught two touchdown passes in that game," Dowler recalled. "It was meaningful. It was so meaningful because it was third-and-short, third-and-a-foot from midfield, [Starr] called a play-action pass. And it was sixteen degrees below zero and the wind was blowing. We were only ahead 7–0. If we make it work, if we play and we execute and do what we needed to do, which took the offensive line to block and the backs to make a good fake and him to throw a good ball and me to get where I needed to get to make it work, and we all did. Fourteen points in that game was pretty significant. If you look back on it, if we don't make that work then we punt. We don't score. The score is still 7–0. ... That game, that play for me was the most meaningful one of our time there with coach Lombardi."

Bowman also lauds Dowler's performance. Ironically, his presence on that final drive was minimal after his head slammed to the icy turf early on, forcing him to leave the game.

"That was guy I always marveled at, who really kept us in that ballgame," Bowman recalled. "I don't know why more people never picked up on that. Boyd is kind of the prototype of today's wide receivers. He was six-five and could run and without him we don't win that game."

With a mixture of bemusement and pride, Bowman also includes himself among the game's unsung heroes.

"Boyd and myself, we were the guys who shot Liberty Valance," Bowman said, referencing a 1960s John Wayne movie in which credit for a major accomplishment went to someone else.

In the Cowboys locker room, there remained a sense if disbelief, anguish, and exhaustion.

Defensive tackle Jethro Pugh, who had the best shot at stopping Starr's lunge, shook his head at the audaciousness of that final call.

"It wasn't a smart call," he said. "But it worked. That's what good teams do."

What he left unsaid at the moment was the belief he maintained until his dying day that Kramer's hand came up from his three-point stance an instant before the ball was snapped, which would have, and probably should have, been an offside penalty.

How would the game have been remembered if the Packers faced fourth down from the 6-yard-line as opposed to the two-foot line?

Pugh was convinced Kramer left early because he hit Pugh so quickly it seemed almost unbelievable.

Bowman, the lineman next to Kramer, has never been sure one way or the other if his linemate was offside.

"It was never called," he said.

But Lilly was certain. So was Jordan.

"Of course he was offsides," Jordan said.

"I think he was offsides," Lilly said. "But it really wouldn't have mattered because we were standing on ice anyway. I don't think anyone would have gotten to Bart."

Pugh also credited Bowman with the key block that moved him just far enough away from Starr to allow the quarterback to squeeze into the end zone.

Lilly, who had been with the Cowboys since their inception and had suffered through the winless seasons and the mediocrity, agonized over those final four minutes as well.

"The Packers were just so well disciplined on that drive," he recalled. "They ran the perfect plays. And I remember on the 1-yard line, the Packers called a timeout and we tried to dig in to get some footing, but the ground was frozen. Really and truly, if we'd had any brains at all we would have called a timeout of our own. We had already talked about using a screwdriver and digging a hole and that would have given us a push. Our equipment guy, Jack Eskridge, was all set to do it, but he didn't do it."

Decades later, Lilly insisted he and his fellow defenders expected the quarterback sneak even if the call surprised just about everyone else on both sidelines.

"They did exactly what I would have done," Lilly said. "I absolutely did expect the quarterback sneak and we tried to get as low as we could, but with that frozen ground it was like spinning your wheels. [Linebacker] Chuck Howley came over the top and almost got there, but he just couldn't get there."

Linebacker Lee Roy Jordan also recalled that even though they knew it was coming, the defense would have to perform perfectly to stop it.

"I was lined up over the fullback [Chuck Mercein], and I had two responsibilities—tackle the fullback if he got the ball, or tackle the quarterback if he was going to try and sneak it in," he said. "So they double-teamed Jethro Pugh, and once Bart took his jab step back, he was over the goal line, and there was nothing we could about it. Everyone knew it was coming."

Not everyone, as it turned out.

"It wasn't a good call but now it's a great call," Landry said in a postgame interview. "I thought Starr would roll and, depending on what he saw, throw to an open receiver or just toss the ball out of bounds to stop the clock and give them time to get [kicker Don Chandler] on the field. If the play they ran had failed, the game would have been over. There's no way they would have gotten off another play."

Cowboys defensive line coach Ermal Allen was even more blunt.

"I just wish it had failed," he said. "You think there wouldn't have been a few million words written about that? Then we'd see how smart [Lombardi] felt."

But it did succeed and the results reverberated around the NFL. In fact, Lombardi's reputation, which had already reached mythical levels, was elevated even further by what many saw as the ultimate gamble by the ultimate gambler.

And now his Packers had the three straight NFL titles he had so coveted. Against the odds and despite the kinds of injuries that would have crippled and destroyed most teams, the Packers had battled the elements and the younger, stronger Dallas Cowboys and prevailed.

That should have been enough but, of course, it wasn't.

Two weeks down the road, the Packer still had to play the AFL champion Oakland Raiders in Super Bowl II. And immediately after that game of games, it wasn't exactly a topic the Packers were eager to think about.

"The Cowboys game had been so emotional and taken so much out of us," Starr recalled. "It took us a long time to get ready for the Super Bowl."

To most of the football-watching nation, not to mention players from both the winning NFL champion Packers and the defeated Cowboys, what had transpired on Lambeaus Field's frozen turf had for all intents and purposes been the championship game of professional football.

Sure, the NFL and AFL had merged into one entity the year before, and in theory the two leagues were on equal footing. But to those who knew football, the chasm between the NFL and the upstart AFL was still a mile wide.

The Packers had proven that the season before by dismantling the Kansas City Chiefs in the first Super Bowl. The Packers had put on a desultory performance in that game, using spurts of superb play to distance themselves from the scrappy Chiefs, who desperately wanted to prove they belonged on the same field with the powerful Packers.

Famously, Lombardi was a nervous wreck before that game, knowing that the Packers, who had held off the Cowboys in a terrific game two weeks earlier in Dallas to win the NFL title, were in a no-win situation.

Defeat the AFL champs and they would have only done that they were expected to do. Lose to the upstarts and everything Lombardi had built in Green Bay would be questioned. So he was tense and irritable and uncertain what would transpire.

But in the end, the Packers were workmanlike and professional, everything the Old Man had taught them to be. And in the end, they rolled over the Chiefs, 35–10, in a game that really wasn't even that close.

So now Lombardi had to get this team back up for the AFL's best again. And he knew it would not be easy. The NFL championship game, which had already been dubbed the Ice Bowl, had taken a lot out of his battered, aging crew.

Several players, including linebackers Ray Nitschke and Dave Robinson, running back Donny Anderson, and center Ken Bowman, were dealing with the aftereffects of frostbite. The Packers were emotionally spent as well.

Bart Starr, for example, didn't even know another game had to be played until later in the evening when he saw the Oakland Raiders playing the Houston Oilers for the AFL title in Oakland.

After the drama of the Ice Bowl, yes, there was still another game to be played for the right to play in Super Bowl II in Miami, Florida.

To say the AFL title tilt was an afterthought was to understate the obvious. For all the drama of the Packers-Cowboys game, the Raiders-Oilers game operated well under the national radar.

On a 45 degree afternoon in Oakland, the Raiders overwhelmed the Oilers, 40–7. Hewritt Dixon rushed for 144 yards and Pete Banaszak added another 116 and the Raiders defense forced three turnovers while holding Houston to 146 total yards to post an easy win.

In fairness, the Raiders were clearly the class of the AFL that season, posting a 13–1 record and boasting the league's best defense. It was a young and strong defense that allowed an average of just 235 yards per game and had intercepted 30 passes, the second-highest total in the AFL.

On offense, the Raiders relied on the running of Dixon, Banaszak, and Clem Daniels, averaging 138 yards per game on the ground. But they also had the league's MVP, quarterback Daryle Lamonica, who was nicknamed the "Mad Bomber" and who had thrown for 3,228 yards and 30 touchdowns.

So, for the Packers it was a time to take a breath and go back to work knowing that, as it was the year before, a win over the AFL was necessary to seal the legitimacy of what they'd already accomplished

But for several veteran players, something felt different this time around. Lombardi was more circumspect as the game approached. His instructions were low key and general, as if the need to yell instructions was no longer necessary. After all, if his players didn't know what to do by now, chances are they weren't going to learn it now.

Rumors had begun to swirl shortly after the Ice Bowl that Lombardi was thinking of stepping down as head coach. Some media reports suggested Lombardi would give up the head coaching duties, handing the duties over to his longtime defensive coordinator Phil Bengtson, while maintaining his role as general manager. Both jobs, Lombardi had determined, were simply too much.

And while both the Packers and Lombardi denied any imminent changes, the feeling among the players was unmistakable. And it was all true. In fact, the night after beating the Cowboys in the Ice Bowl, Lombardi had told his son, Vince Jr., that he had just coached his next-to-last game as Green Bay's head coach.

But Lombardi, ever the master manipulator, wanted to keep it all secret so as not to distract his team from its preparation for the Super Bowl.

But the rumors grew, and finally in the Packers' final film session on Friday night prior to the game with the Raiders, Lombardi let the news slip—sort of.

After the film session, he snapped off the projector and said, "This may be the last time we'll be together, so . . ." That's all he could say as emotion overtook him.

Most of the younger players didn't put two and two together, assuming the coach was simply talking about this being the last teamwide session of a long season.

But several veterans knew this was something more.

Jerry Kramer had played for Lombardi for ten years and he had grown up with him. Lombardi had pushed Kramer hard and relentlessly and Kramer was convinced that without Lombardi he would not have made it in the NFL. His relationship with Lombardi was special and deep and lasting and, even fifty years later, he speaks in reverential tones of the coach who made him who he is.

Kramer knew that Super Bowl II was going to be the finale for the coach and, perhaps more important and in the way only players can know, that this was likely the end of an era.

So in the Orange Bowl locker room prior to the last game Vince Lombardi would coach the Packers, the emotions of a team took over.

Linebacker Ray Nitschke, still in pain from the frostbite in his feet suffered from the Ice Bowl stood up and said simply, "Men, let's play with our hearts."

Defensive end Willie Davis, whose career was resurrected thanks to a trade that brought him to Green Bay from Cleveland, said, "We've got to win this game because there's no way I'm prepared to explain how we lost."

Kramer also stood and said, "Let's win one for the Old Man."

Later, Kramer said, "I wanted to play a perfect game for my coach."

And the Green Bay dynasty roared one last time, beating the Oakland Raiders, 33–14. It was not dominating, and it was not pretty, and perhaps on another day, the Raiders would have been good enough to beat the Packers—but not on this day.

The team that had prided itself over the years on playing without the cumbersome baggage of emotion played with all the emotion it could muster. Bart Starr, who too had sensed days earlier that his coach would coach them no more, threw for 202 yards and a touchdown and was named the game's MVP for the second straight year.

But even though it was his last game as Packers head coach, Lombardi remained very much in control. Sensing it as time to try something different, Lombardi tabbed Ben Wilson, a 6-foot-1, 230-pounder he had traded with the Los Angeles Rams for that previous summer in an effort to fill Jim Taylor's enormous void.

Wilson had played well all season when called upon, rushing for 453 yards, which was second-best on the team behind Jim Grabowski.

But late-season injuries nagged Wilson, prompting Lombardi to acquire Mercein. Wilson played sparingly in the playoffs, carrying the ball just three times in the Ice Bowl. But with two weeks to heal up, Lombardi decided Wilson provided the Packers with more options in the backfield.

As a result, Wilson got the call to start at fullback in place of the Ice Bowl hero Mercein, who the previous week had his photo on the cover of *Sports Illustrated*.

It was vintage Lombardi and it ended up being the right move.

Wilson rushed for 62 yards and Donny Anderson added another 48 yards and a touchdown against the Raiders. Herb Adderley also returned an interception for a touchdown and Boyd Dowler caught a 62-yard touchdown pass.

As for Mercein, the toast of Green Bay and of the everyman everywhere, he carried the ball just one time.

"I understood," Mercein said, even though years later he still really didn't.

Workmanlike, efficient, and effective, the Packers had played in pro football's first two Super Bowls and won them both with relative ease. And as the clock hit 0:00 at the Orange Bowl, Kramer instinctively lifted Lombardi on his shoulders. The iconic photo of Kramer looking up at his coach is one of the truly memorable images of what Lombardi meant to the Packers and what the Packers meant to the coach.

"It's something I thought would be appropriate," Kramer said afterward of the spontaneous gesture, something the Packers had never done in all of Lombardi's years in Green Bay. "All he said was, 'Let's head to the locker room, boys.'"

And in the locker room afterward, this veteran Packers team, which had been through so much over the years and battled through so much just that season, rose as one and gave Lombardi a standing ovation.

Kramer remembers as if were just yesterday.

"It was like a four- or five-minute ovation," he said. "We all understood. We knew it was over and we were saying thank you. We all knew it was the end of something and also the beginning of something."

But they all knew what had been would be no longer. A dynasty, as all dynasties must, was ending and it was bittersweet and sad and inevitable.

"We really were the dominant team of the 1960s," said center Ken Bowman. "But it was the end of an era for the Green Bay Packers, and I think we all knew it."

Just a few weeks later, Lombardi made official what everyone already knew—he was stepping down as head coach and anointing Phil Bengtson, who had been with him from the start in Green Bay, as the Packers new head coach. Lombardi would stay on general manager.

Most people accepted Lombardi's reasoning for stepping away from coaching. He was exhausted from handling both jobs as head coach and general manager, and it was time for some else to coach.

But, again, it was the veteran players who knew it was something more. Lombardi had been battling digestive problems for years, and players had grown accustomed to seeing him carrying a bottle of antacid with him. He was hurting and beyond tired and needed to try and slow down.

Bengtson would carry on much of what Lombardi had preached, and the old coach would still be on hand to select talent.

But the players knew everything had changed.

"I think we lost our heartbeat," Boyd Dowler said soon after. "We knew it wasn't our time anymore. Our time had passed."

In truth, while Lombardi had burned out as coach, he also read the same writing on the wall that everyone else was seeing. These Packers were tired and old and done. The dynasty had reached its end, and he did not want to stick around to see the aftermath.

Indeed, in 1968, with much of the same roster that had won three straight NFL titles and the first two Super Bowls, the Packers sputtered to a 6–7–1 record, their first losing season since the 1–10–1 disaster of 1958 that led the Packers organization to hire Lombardi in the first place. The Packers would not return to the playoffs until 1972, would not win another playoff game until 1982, nor win another Super Bowl until 1996.

Lombardi stayed in his role as Green Bay's general manager for just one long, frustrating season. He would watch practice and pace incessantly, seeing mistakes that needed correcting and desperately wanting to offer guidance and make changes but knowing he could not and, more important, should not.

He watched as Bengtson, tall and laconic and the antithesis of the old coach, ran his practices far differently than he did. Lombardi often complained he never had enough time to do everything that needed to be done when he was the head coach. Now, he had too much time on his hands and he was learning that was far worse.

As the 1968 season approached, he famously had the Lambeau Field press box, where he would sit during games, soundproofed so the reporters could not hear his volcanic reaction to just about everything he saw transpiring on the field.

Before that season was over, he realized that, perhaps, he had made a mistake stepping away and when the Washington Redskins approached with him an attractive offer as head coach, general manager, and part-owner of a franchise that looked remarkably like the Packers did in 1959 when he took over.

There was talent there, but no focus, no vision, no history. It was an irresistible opportunity that Lombardi could not refuse.

So in early February 1968, he left a team and a town and state heartbroken for a new opportunity. And Lombardi did in Washington what he had done in Green Bay, taking a franchise that had not had a winning season since 1955 and leading it to a 7–5–2 mark in 1969. It seemed a new day had dawned in Washington but less than a year later, Lombardi was dead from cancer.

If an era had not ended before, it surely was over now.

But as one dynasty ended, another was stirring in Dallas.

The Cowboys had built themselves haltingly and carefully in their first few years. They had used the draft wisely, made smart trades, brought in players from other teams who fit the way the Cowboys wanted to play.

And they had paid attention to what the Packers had done.

"We learned a lot about ourselves by playing the Packers," said halfback Dan Reeves. "We saw how they approached the game and we knew that's how we had to do it."

He recalled a 1965 preseason game when he was just a rookie and the Cowboys played the Packers in what amounted to meaningless contest.

"The thing that got my attention was that on punts their defense stayed on the field," he said. "I couldn't believe it. I had Ray Nitschke on me in a preseason game and I said, 'Where is this thing going?' I couldn't believe it. They kept their starting offense and defense out there for special teams and that told me a lot. That told me that everything mattered. Everything, no matter how small it seemed. When we played the Packers, we said, 'This is where we wanted to be.' It was a great measuring stick."

As it turns out, it was also pure Lombardi. From their days as assistant coaches in New York, there was an unspoken rivalry between the two men. Both were strong-willed and in possession of massive egos though obviously they had different ways of showing it.

It was especially important to Lombardi that he remain just a little bit ahead of his colleague and that meant beating him at every opportunity. To Lombardi, it did not matter if it was a championship game or a meaningless preseason game—it was an opportunity to beat Landry and he took every one of them seriously.

And now they had played back-to-back NFL championship games, losing the first by just seven points and the second by only four, and they knew they had chances to win both of those games. Still, they used those losses to the Packers to measure themselves.

The Ice Bowl, in particular, had stayed with many of the Cowboys throughout the long offseason. The game had been there for the taking. They had the NFL's best, the gold standard for how to play the game the right way, on the ropes and let them up. The Packers went 68 yards on an ice rink of a field in the final four minutes and somehow pulled out the victory.

For proud veteran defensive tackle Bob Lilly, the loss in Green Bay was especially difficult.

"That loss broke our hearts," he said. "It was a very tough loss for us and it affected me into the next year."

But while the Packers were reeling from the loss of their coach and foundation, the Cowboys were set. They had Landry on top of the pyramid, an offense that remained dynamic and the "Doomsday Defense" all but untouched. With the experience of two straight championship losses to build on, the Cowboys seemed to be the team to beat in the NFL.

And they proved it early in the 1968 season, roaring out to a 6-0 record and outscoring their opposition 213–64. In what seemed to be perfect symmetry, that set up an October game in Dallas with the red-hot Cowboys facing the sputtering 2–3–1 Packers. It would not make up for what had happened the previous two seasons, but this game would be a showcase of how the Cowboys had improved and the Packers, well, had not.

There was a new kid in town and the Cowboys were ready to prove it.

But a funny thing happened on the way to that decisive lesson. The Packers played superbly. Bart Starr threw for 260 yards and four touchdowns, and Green Bay's defense forced four turnovers on the way to a 28–17 Packers victory.

And the Cowboys learned, again, that dynasties don't die easily.

Dallas went on to post a 12–2 regular season record but again came up short in the postseason, this time falling to the Cleveland Browns, 31–20, in a game called 51 seconds before it finished because the Cleveland crowd had spilled onto the field in celebration.

The frustration continued the following year when the Cowboys again win their conference but, in the first round of the playoffs, again were ousted by the Browns, this time by a score of 38–14.

Finally, the Cowboys found the key to success and it would signal one of the most successful runs in the history of the NFL.

Starting in 1970, the Cowboys not only succeeded in the playoffs but reached Super Bowl V, losing in the final seconds to the Baltimore Colts. Dallas would reach the Super Bowl five times in the next nine seasons, winning twice. They would also reach the postseason fourteen of the next sixteen seasons, earning them the moniker "America's Team" along the way.

And the one constant through it all was Tom Landry, who despite seeing a changing NFL landscape as well as a changing nation, maintained what he knew worked.

The Cowboys and Packers have met six times in the playoffs since that frigid Sunday afternoon in Green Bay when players from both teams knew what survival really meant.

The Cowboys won the first four meetings —all played in Dallas—in 1982 and then again in three straight years from 1993 to '95 when it became clear that another Cowboys dynasty was ending and a new one, led by a bash gunslinger at quarterback named Brett Favre, was rising again in Green Bay.

In 2014 and again 2016 the Packers again beat the Cowboys in the playoffs, this time with another star at quarterback, Aaron Rodgers.

But with all the history that has rolled by since 1967, the subject is never far away.

The Cowboys and Packers. The Ice Bowl. Linked forever and always.

8

THE LEGACY

ON JANUARY 12, 1997, the Green Bay Packers played in a league championship game for the first time since the Ice Bowl, nearly thirty years earlier.

Much had changed over the years but, then again, very little had changed.

The game would be played at Lambeau Field, but it was played in a stadium and in a city and as part of an NFL that bore little resemblance to what had transpired all those years earlier.

Lambeau Field had been expanded in the intervening years to more than 60,000 seats. Heated, enclosed luxury boxes had been added as had a modern scoreboard with all the bells and whistles. Ringing the inside of the stadium was the Ring of Honor, heralding some of the great players who had played for the Packers over the years. Many of those names—Starr, Nitschke, Davis, Lombardi—had been part of a game that had changed a franchise and a sport forever.

Green Bay had grown from a sleepy small city in northeast Wisconsin to a little bit bigger though perhaps a little bit less sleepy city. Packers fans had been through all this before. The old-timers, the ones who really had attended the Ice Bowl or listened to Ted Moore on the radio or Ray Scott's play by play on TV, remember that the '67 game was every bit as important as a new generation of fans were looking at the '96 game.

But so much had changed.

The quarterback, Brett Favre, was a brash, talented force of nature with the kind of arm that could throw a pass through three defenders one play and then throw an interception to one of those defenders the next play.

He did not manage games like Bart Starr did. To manage a game was to relinquish control and Favre would never do that.

But the kid could play and since taking over as the Packers' quarterback in 1992, he had held Green Bay and Packers fans in the palm of his hand. He could no wrong, even when he was doing wrong.

This was a team built by a clever, relentless, sometimes ruthless general manager, Ron Wolf, who was told by friends five years earlier, when the job was offered to him, to turn it down.

"You can't win there," he was told. "Watch me" was his response.

So he built a team the way he was convinced would succeed. All he needed was time.

The coach was the antithesis of the fire-breathing autocracy of Lombardi. Mike Holmgren, like Lombardi, had paid his dues first as a high school coach and then in the junior college ranks before hooking up with offensive wizard Bill Walsh with the San Francisco 49ers.

Like Lombardi, Holmgren was an offensive guru, committed to the precision and attention to detail that his offense required. Practice properly, he said, and you'll do the job right when it matters in a game.

Like Lombardi, Holmgren was an assistant coach in demand in 1992, and several NFL teams were trying to lure the big Californian to their franchise. But Wolf convinced Holmgren that Green Bay was the place to be. He brought up the history and the personnel and the plan and he showed him the spot where Bart Starr scored the touchdown no Packers fan would ever forget.

That did the trick.

And, like Lombardi, this new Packers regime would have to slog through too many years of mediocrity to turn the franchise around.

When the two men began their partnership in 1992, they faced a recent Packers history that was, to say the least, daunting, Since the Ice Bowl season of 1967, the Packers had managed five winning seasons, one division title, two trips to the playoffs, and one playoff victory.

Much as it had been before Lombardi took over in 1959, Green Bay had once again become the place no player wanted to go.

In 1993, Wolf signed the most coveted player in the NFL's new free agency system, former Eagles defensive end Reggie White. His signing by Green Bay, which beat out the likes of the powerhouse Washington Redskins and San Francisco 49ers among others, stunned the NFL and changed the culture and perception of Packers.

White often reveled in telling a story every player of that era understood only too well.

"My coaches in Philadelphia always threatened guys by saying that if they didn't straighten up, he'd be sent to Green Bay," White recalled. "Nobody wanted that."

Of course, a boatload of money and the chance to play for a young, improving, exciting team showed White and other free agents over the years, that Green Bay may not have been the end of the world after all.

And steadily, the Packers did indeed improve and Favre, White, and a cast of supporting talent led the Packers to the best record in the NFL in 1996 and on this cold, clear day, a chance to go back to the Super Bowl.

Of course, many of the players taking part in this 1996 NFC Champiomnship Game had not even been born when Bart Starr snuck into the end zone with 13 seconds to play to beat the Dallas Cowboys all those years ago. Those who were around likely knew nothing of the game until later years when football became so important in their lives. And as their football education grew, especially as a Green Bay Packer, they realized any understanding of the game of football had to include knowledge of the Ice Bowl and everything it meant.

In an almost karmic irony, I appeared more than likely that the Packers would once again meet the Dallas Cowboys for the NFC championship and the right to play in Super Bowl XXXI.

The Cowboys and Packers, not unlike thirty years earlier, were coming into the playoffs as two of the league's best teams. The Packers rolled to the NFC Central title with a 13–3 record and the Cowboys had again won the NFC East with a 10–6 mark.

Thirty years earlier, the Packers had been a dynasty on its final fumes. Age and injury had decimated the once-proud Packers, and they were seen as a team on the decline. But they had something, somewhere in the frigid air of Wisconsin and beaten the young, exuberant, and powerful Cowboys. Then the Packers won their second Super Bowl as the final roar of a champion. And they had not been back since.

Now the tables were turned.

The Cowboys, in the first season after Tom Landry was let go in 1989, had hit rock bottom, finishing 1–15 with a team to rookies and unknown veterans.

But coach Jimmy Johnson had stayed patient and aggressive and arrogant and three years later, his Cowboys were back on top. He led them to Super Bowls titles in 1992 and 1993 and when Johnson was replaced by Barry Switzer in 1994, there was a still enough talent to squeeze out yet another Super Bowl championship in 1995.

But like those Packers of 1967, the Cowboys of 1996 were breaking down. Their top players, quarterback Troy Aikman and running back Emmitt Smith, and much of a dominant defense was on the other side of the mountain. Still, maybe, like the Packers of yore, the Cowboys had one more miracle left.

And it certainly seemed like the case when, in the wild-card playoff game, the Cowboys overwhelmed the Minnesota Vikings, 40–15, setting up a second-round game against the young, brash, but untested Carolina Panthers, who would be playing their first postseason game.

The matchup everyone in the league wanted was close. All the Cowboys had to do was beat the overmatched Panthers and Green Bay had to take care of the San Francisco 49ers. If that happened, it would be the fourth straight year the Packers and Cowboys would meet in the playoffs and provide a chance to—dare it be said?—set up Ice Bowl II.

The Packers did their part, swamping the 49ers in a cold, driving rainstorm at Lambeau Field. But in a stunner, the Cowboys dynasty came to a crashing end as the Panthers dominated Dallas with a 26–17 victory. The Cowboys are still waiting for another trip to the Super Bowl.

The Panthers' unexpected victory sent Packers fans into a black depression. This was the year, they were convinced, that the Packers would exact revenge on the team that had eliminated their heroes from the playoffs the previous three years.

Even the Panthers understood.

"I know Packers fans wanted the Cowboys," said Carolina quarterback Kerry Collins. "I understand that completely because it's become such a great rivalry. But you know what? We beat the Cowboys and we're here."

And the Packers understood only too well.

"They're a good team and they deserve to be here," said Packers' defensive end Reggie White.

Even without the Cowboys coming to Lambeau Feld, the Ice Bowl parallels were eerie.

Thirty years earlier, the Lambeau Field turf had been the subject of some consternation when Lombardi's pride and joy heating system malfunctioned, turning the playing surface into an ice rink.

In 1997, the field condition was again an issue.

In the win over the 49ers, played in a deluge, the field had been badly torn up. In fact, when NFL officials toured the field on the Monday before the championship game, it was deemed just a step above a cow pasture.

So the league invested $150,000 to have forty truckloads of Maryland sod transported to Green Bay for a major refurbishing project.

All week, as the nation's sports media gathered to chronicle the run up to the game, along with interviewing coaches and quarterbacks and linebackers, the Packers' head groundskeeper was asked to report progress on the field.

And in another move that might have only worked in Green Bay, the old sod was removed put in jars, labeled "Frozen Tundra" and sold to raise money for local charities. The sod sold out in four hours and raised $200,000.

Finally, there was the weather on game day.

While the players thirty years earlier had been stunned to awake to minus-13 degree temperatures, weather forecasting was infinitely better in 1997. Everyone knew early that week how cold it would be. And it would be cold—the game-time temperature was three degrees with a wind chill of minus-17.

Bob Lilly and Dan Reeves and Bob Hayes and Ray Nitschke and Bart Starr and Willie Davis would have smiled if they'd been able to play in weather that "warm."

And, just as it had been years before, the fans came in droves despite the cold. The attendance was 60,216 (there were only 574 no-shows) and the steam that rose from stands hearkened back to the hearty souls who braved the Ice Bowl.

The result? After a slow start, the Packers battered the Panthers, 30–13, to earn their first trip to the Super Bowl since 1967. There would be no late quarterback sneak, no second-guessing about calls, no final epic drive.

And as the jubilant Packers ran around the field celebrating with fans, the ghosts of the past were everywhere.

Paul Hornung, who had played for the Packers when they were so bad that he considered retiring before Lombardi showed up, was on hand as an honorary captain and was weeping afterward.

Ray Nitschke had remained loyal to the Packers even after he had been unceremoniously ousted from his starting linebacker job in 1972. He was there to and saw his team return to greatness. Less than two years later he died of a heart attack at age sixty-one.

And, of course, Lombardi's spirit was everywhere. Five years earlier, a Milwaukee newspaper conducted a reader poll asking who the greatest coach in Packers history was. Lombardi came in second to Lindy Infante, a coach who had led the Packers to a 10–6 record the year before.

That seemed long ago and far away now.

After an awful 1991 season, the Packers hired Ron Wolf as general manager and gave him the kind of powers no general manager for the team had enjoyed since the days of Lombardi.

Lombardi needed three years to turn the Packers into world champs. Wolf needed six.

And has he stood watching the Packers celebrate with their fans on that frigid day, he too wept.

"This place is hallowed ground," he said simply.

This was a Packers team that Vince Lombardi would have loved—strong and smart and committed to doing the little things the right way, they had lived up their considerable potential and reached the top.

And the journey was completed two weeks later in New Orleans when they defeated the New England Patriots for their third Super Bowl title. And the trophy, named for the Packers' legendary coach, was coming home.

In an emotional speech to his team after the game, Packers coach Mike Holmgren said it best.

"As much as this means to every other team," said Holmgren, holding high the Vince Lombardi Trophy. "It means more to us."

Players from both the Green Bay Packers and Dallas Cowboys understand only too well the history of the franchises for which they play.

It's everywhere, permeating not only the NFL but professional sports. Even football fans who claim to other allegiances look at the Cowboys and Packers, perhaps grudgingly, as part of the NFL's royalty.

Through the 2016 season, the Cowboys, since their creation in 1960, have won 22 division titles, played in eight Super Bowls and won five of them.

The Packers, charter members of the National Football League in 1922, have won 19 division titles, claimed 13 world championships, played in five Super Bowls and won four through 2016.

The Cowboys and Packers have also combined to put thirty-nine players or coaches into the Pro Football Hall of Fame and, incredibly, fourteen participated in the Ice Bowl, including both head coaches.

For both franchises, the Ice Bowl remains the eternal connection.

"I think the game is still important for many different reasons," said center Ken Bowman. "It was the last game for coach Lombardi, or next to last. He was a legendary coach coaching his last game for a legendary team. It also captured a time in America and captured most of the American public. Red Auerbach was the coach of the best team in the NBA, the Boston Celtics. They were the team to beat in pro basketball and then there was coach Lombardi and the Packers were the team to beat in pro football. We were a tough team to beat and everyone knew it. And most of that was due to coach Lombardi. He had a winning personality and a winning philosophy."

Even today and now in his seventies, Ken Bowman has always looked at his time with the Green Bay Packers in something less than a romantic way.

But he thinks he has put his finger on why the Packers meant so, and still mean so much, to the NFL and pro sports in general.

"You have this little town in northern Wisconsin," he said. "You have 100,000 people there or something like that and they're playing teams in Chicago and New York and Los Angeles, teams with millions of people in those cities. In most people's eyes, it's a romance of the concept of the little guy who can't win. He can't compete. He can't succeed. But the Packers have shown that isn't true. He can compete and he did succeed. That's powerful."

The game was played fifty years ago. That's half a century and the world and America and Dallas, Texas and Green Bay, Wisconsin have changed a lot.

But one important thing hasn't changed. Through the 2016 season, both the Cowboys and Packers remain among the elite in the NFL. Indeed, the two teams met one more time in the playoffs in 2016, with the Packers pulling out a last-second victory to upset the favored Cowboys. It was just one more chapter in the story of two franchises that always seem to do something dramatic when they get together.

The names have changed and, yes, many are now gone.

Don Meredith, Jethro Pugh, Bob Hayes, Willie Townes, and Tom Landry are among the Cowboys who have passed away while the Packers have mourned the losses of Ray Nitschke , Max McGee, Henry Jordan, Elijah Pitts, Travis Williams, Lionel Aldridge, and, of course Vince Lombardi.

And those who remain still get asked about the Ice Bowl.

"All the time," Reeves said with a laugh.

"I didn't even play that much and I get asked about it," said Dallas fullback Walt Garrison.

"I was injured and didn't even play," said Cowboys center Dave Manders. "The only thing I got out of that game was a bad cold. But it was still incredible to be part of it."

"My kids said I should get royalties for all the time that game has been shown TV," said Chuck Mercein, the unlikeliest of heroes. "It was a great honor to be a part of it."

Most of the players who took part in the drama that was the Ice Bowl have kept a piece of it for themselves, unwilling to reveal everything about a game that everyone thinks they know.

But the fraternity, always small in the best of times, is even smaller now and the memories grow ever more narrow as time goes by.

But they all know they were part of something special, something memorable and something that, in the annals of American sports will never be forgotten.

"Every year they show it," said Dan Reeves, who pauses ever so slightly. "And the game has a name."

Yes it does. And it always will.

APPENDIX

DALLAS COWBOYS 1967 ROSTER

George Andrie	DE	6-7	250	Marquette
Craig Baynham	E	6-1	205	Georgia Tech
Jim Boeke	T	6-5	260	Heidelberg
Phil Clark	DB	6-2	210	Northwestern
Frank Clarke	E	6-1	210	Colorado
Mike Connelly	OL	6-3	250	Utah State
Dick Daniels	DB	5-9	180	Pacific
Leon Donohue	G	6-4	245	San Jose State
Dave Edwards	LB	6-1	230	Auburn
Mike Gaechter	DB	6-0	190	Oregon
Walt Garrison	FB	6-0	205	Oklahoma State
Pete Gent	E	6-4	205	Michigan State
Cornell Green	DB	6-3	210	Utah State
Bob Hayes	E	5-11	185	Florida A&M
Chuck Howley	LB	6-2	225	West Virginia

Mike Johnson	DB	5-11	185	Kansas
Lee Roy Jordan	LB	6-1	225	Alabama
Bob Lilly	DT	6-5	260	Texas Christian
Tony Liscio	T	6-5	255	Tulsa
Dave Manders	C	6-2	250	Michigan State
Don Meredith	QB	6-3	205	Southern Methodist
Craig Morton	QB	6-4	215	California
Ralph Neely	T	6-6	265	Oklahoma
John Niland	G	6-3	245	Iowa
Pettis Norman	TE	6-3	225	Johnson C. Smith
Don Perkins	FB	5-10	200	New Mexico
Jethro Pugh	DT	6-6	260	Elizabeth City State
Dan Reeves	HB	6-1	200	South Carolina
Mel Renfro	S	6-0	190	Oregon
Lance Rentzel	FL	6-2	200	Oklahoma
Jerry Rhome	QB	6-0	185	Tulsa
Les Shy	HB	6-1	200	Long Beach State
Larry Stephens	DT	6-3	250	Texas
Sims Stokes	SE	6-1	200	Northern Arizona
Willie Townes	DE	6-4	260	Tulsa
Danny Villanueva	K/P	5-11	200	New Mexico State
Malcolm Walker	T	6-4	250	Rice
John Wilbur	G	6-3	240	Stanford
Rayfield Wright	T	6-6	260	Fort Valley State

GREEN BAY PACKERS 1967 ROSTER

Herb Adderley	DB	6-0	200	Michigan State
Lionel Aldridge	DE	6-4	245	Utah State
Donny Anderson	RB	6-3	210	Texas Tech
Ken Bowman	C	6-3	230	Wisconsin
Zeke Bratkowski	QB	6-3	210	Georgia
Robert Brown	DT	6-5	260	Arkansas-Pine Bluff
Tom Brown	DB	6-1	195	Maryland
Lee Roy Caffey	LB	6-3	250	Texas A&M
Dick Capp	TE	6-3	235	Boston College
Don Chandler	K	6-2	210	Florida

Tommy Crutcher	LB	6-3	230	Texas Christian
Carroll Dale	WR	6-3	210	Virginia Tech
Willie Davis	DE	6-3	245	Grambling
Boyd Dowler	WR	6-5	225	Colorado
Jim Flanigan	LB	6-3	240	Pittsburgh
Marv Fleming	TE	6-4	245	Utah
Gale Gillingham	OG	6-3	255	Minnesota
Jim Grabowski	RB	6-2	220	Illinois
Forrest Gregg	OT	6-4	250	Southern Methodist
Doug Hart	DB	6-0	190	Texas-Arlington
Don Horn	QB	6-2	195	San Diego State
Bob Hyland	C	6-5	250	Boston College
Bob Jeter	DB	6-1	205	Iowa
Henry Jordan	DT	6-3	250	Virginia
Ron Kostelnik	DT	6-4	260	Cincinnati
Jerry Kramer	OG	6-3	245	Idaho
Bob Long	WR	6-3	205	Wichita State
Max McGee	SE	6-3	210	Tulane
Chuck Mercein	RB	6-2	225	Yale
Ray Nitschke	LB	6-3	250	Illinois
Dave Robinson	LB	6-3	240	Penn State
John Rowser	DB	6-1	180	Michigan
Bob Skoronski	OT	6-3	245	Indiana
Bart Starr	QB	6-1	190	Alabama
Fuzzy Thurston	OG	6-1	245	Valparaiso
Jim Weatherwax	DT	6-7	260	Los Angeles State
Travis Williams	RB	6-1	210	Arizona State
Ben Wilson	RB	6-1	230	Southern California
Willie Wood	DB	5-10	190	Southern California
Steve Wright	OT	6-6	250	Alabama

1967 SEASON RESULTS

Dallas Cowboys (Regular season record 9–5)

21	at Cleveland Browns	14
38	New York Giants	24

ICE BOWL '67

13	Los Angeles Rams	35
17	at Washington Redskins	14
14	New Orleans Saints	10
24	at Pittsburgh Steelers	21
14	at Philadelphia Eagles	21
37	Atlanta Falcons	7
27	at New Orleans Saints	10
20	Washington Redskins	27
46	St. Louis Cardinals	21
17	at Baltimore Colts	23
38	Philadelphia Eagles	17
16	at San Francisco 49ers	24

Eastern Conference playoff

52	Cleveland Browns	14

NFL Championship

17	at Green Bay Packers	21

Green Bay Packers (Regular season record 9–4–1)

17	Detroit Lions	17
13	Chicago Bears	10
23	Atlanta Falcons	0
27	at Detroit Lions	17
7	Minnesota Vikings	10
48	at New York Giants	21
31	at St. Louis Cardinals	23
10	at Baltimore Colts	13
55	Cleveland Browns	7
13	San Francisco 49ers	0
17	at Chicago Bears	13
30	at Minnesota Vikings	27
24	at Los Angeles Rams	27
17	Pittsburgh Steelers	24

Western Conference Playoffs

28   Los Angeles Rams   7

NFL Championship

21   Dallas Cowboys   17

Super Bowl II (Miami, Florida)

33   Oakland Raiders   14

DALLAS COWBOYS 1967
INDIVIDUAL SEASON STATISTICS

PASSING

	Comp-Att	Pct.	Yards	TD	Int.
Don Meredith	128-255	50.2	1,834	16	16
Craig Morton	69-137	50.4	978	10	10
Dan Reeves	4-7	57.1	195	2	1
Jerry Rhome	9-18	50.0	86	0	1

RUSHING

	Att.	Yards	Avg.	TD
Don Perkins	201	823	4.1	6
Dan Reeves	173	603	3.5	5
Walt Garrison	24	146	6.1	0
Pettis Norman	9	91	10.1	0
Don Meredith	28	84	3.0	0
Frank Clarke	4	72	18.0	1
Les Shy	17	59	3.5	0
Craig Morton	15	42	2.8	0

ICE BOWL '67

Craig Baynham	3	6	2.0	1
Jerry Rhome	2	−11	−5.5	0
Danny Villanueva	1	−15	−15.0	0

RECEIVING

	Rec	Yards	Avg.	TD
Lance Rentzel	58	996	17.2	8
Bob Hayes	49	998	20.4	10
Dan Reeves	39	490	12.6	6
Pettis Norman	20	220	11.0	2
Don Perkins	18	116	6.4	0
Frank Clarke	9	119	13.2	1
Pete Gent	9	88	9.8	1
Les Shy	3	36	12.0	0
Craig Baynham	3	13	4.3	0
Walt Garrison	2	17	8.5	0

KICKOFF RETURNS

	Ret	Yards	Avg.	TD
Craig Baynham	12	331	27.6	0
Sims Stokes	4	92	23.0	0
Mel Renfro	5	112	22.4	0
Les Shy	5	96	19.2	0
Walt Garrison	20	366	18.3	0
Bob Hayes	1	17	17.0	0

PUNT RETURNS

	Ret	Yards	Avg.	TD
Bob Hayes	24	276	11.5	1
Lance Rentzel	6	45	7.5	0

PUNTING

	Punts	Avg.
Danny Villanueva	67	40.4

KICKING

	PAT Made-Att	FG Made-Att	Pts
Danny Villanueva	32-34	8-19	56
Harold Deters	9-10	1-4	12

INTERCEPTIONS

	Int	Yards	TD
Cornell Green	7	52	0
Mel Renfro	7	38	0
Mike Johnson	5	88	0
Lee Roy Jordan	3	85	1
Dave Edwards	3	34	1
Mike Gaechter	2	0	0
Chuck Howley	1	28	1
Phil Clark	1	6	0

GREEN BAY PACKERS 1967 INDIVIDUAL SEASON STATISTICS

PASSING

	Comp-Att	Pct.	Yards	TD	Int
Bart Starr	115-210	54.8	1,823	9	17
Zeke Bratkowski	53-94	56.4	724	5	9
Don Horn	12-24	50.0	171	1	1
Donny Anderson	1-2	50.0	19	0	0
Elijah Pitts	1-1	100	21	0	0

ICE BOWL '67

RUSHING

	Att	Yards	Avg.	TD
Jim Grabowski	120	466	3.9	2
Ben Wilson	103	453	4.4	2
Donny Anderson	97	402	4.1	6
Elijah Pitts	77	247	3.2	6
Travis Williams	35	188	5.4	1
Bart Starr	21	90	4.3	0
Chuck Mercein	14	56	4.0	1
Carroll Dale	1	9	9.0	0
Zeke Bratkowski	5	6	1.2	0
Don Horn	1	-2	-2.0	0

RECEIVING

	Rec	Yards	Avg	TD
Boyd Dowler	54	836	15.5	4
Carroll Dale	35	738	21.1	5
Donny Anderson	22	231	15.0	3
Elijah Pitts	15	210	14.0	0
Ben Wilson	14	88	6.3	0
Jim Grabowski	12	171	14.3	1
Marv Fleming	10	126	12.6	1
Bob Long	8	96	12.0	0
Travis Williams	5	80	16.0	1
Allen Brown	3	43	14.3	0
Max McGee	3	33	11.0	0
Chuck Mercein	1	6	6.0	0

KICKOFF RETURNS

	Ret	Yards	Avg.	TD
Travis Williams	18	739	41.1	4
Donny Anderson	11	226	20.5	0

Herb Adderley	10	207	20.7	0
Tommy Crutcher	3	48	16.0	0
Allen Brown	1	13	13.0	0
Doug Hart	1	8	8.0	0
Dave Robinson	1	0	0.0	0
Willie Wood	1	0	0.0	0

PUNT RETURNS

	Ret	Yards	Avg.	TD
Donny Anderson	9	98	10.9	0
Tom Brown	9	40	4.4	0
Elijah Pitts	9	16	1.8	0
Willie Wood	12	3	0.3	0

PUNTING

	Punts	Avg.
Donny Anderson	65	36.6
Don Chandler	1	31.0

KICKING

	PAT Made-Att	FG Made-Att	Pts
Don Chandler	39-39	19-39	96
Chuck Mercein	2-3	0-1	2

INTERCEPTIONS

	No.	Yards	TD
Bob Jeter	8	78	0
Willie Wood	4	60	0
Herb Adderley	4	16	1
Dave Robinson	4	16	0

Ray Nitschke	3	35	1
Lee Roy Caffey	2	28	0
Tom Brown	1	51	0

1967 DALLAS COWBOYS SEASON TEAM STATISTICS

	Dallas	Opponents
FIRST DOWNS	261	236
By Rushing	109	64
By Passing	141	145
By Penalty	11	27
RUSHING YARDAGE		
Rushes	477	339
Yards	1,900	1,081
Average per rush	4.0	3.2
Touchdowns	13	11
PASSING		
Attempts	417	482
Completions	210	260
Comp. Pct.	50.4	53.9
Yards	3,093	3,167
Sacked	42	45
Yards lost sacked	294	377
Net Yards passing	2,799	2,790
Touchdowns	28	21
Interceptions	28	29
Pct. Int	6.7	6.0
PUNTING		
Punts	67	72
Avg.	40.4	42.5

PUNT RETURNS		
Returns	33	37
Yards	320	266
Avg. Yards	9.7	7.2
Touchdowns	1	0
KICKOFF RETURNS		
Returns	48	59
Yards	1,014	1,350
Avg. Yards	21.1	22.9
Touchdowns	0	0
INTERCEPTION RETURNS		
Interceptions	29	28
Yards	331	353
Avg. Yards	11.4	12.6
Touchdowns	3	3
PENALTIES		
Penalties	81	64
Yards	785	717
FUMBLES		
Fumbles	26	27
Fumbles lost	14	19
SCORING		
Points	342	268
XP attempted	44	35
XP made	41	34
FG attempted	23	23
FG made	9	8
Pct. FG made	39.1	34.8
Safeties	2	0

1967 GREEN BAY PACKERS TEAM STATISTICS

	GB	Opponents
FIRST DOWNS	243	183
By Rushing	115	98
By Passing	112	78
By Penalty	16	7
RUSHING YARDAGE		
Rushes	474	443
Yards	1,915	1,923
Average per rush	4.0	4.3
Touchdowns	18	7
PASSING		
Attempts	331	337
Completions	182	155
Comp. Pct.	55.0	46.0
Yards	2,758	1,644
Sacked	41	29
Yards lost sacked	394	267
Net Yards passing	2,364	1,377
Touchdowns	15	13
Interceptions	27	26
Pct. Int	8.2	7.7
PUNTING		
Punts	66	75
Avg.	36.5	41.6
PUNT RETURNS		
Returns	39	13
Yards	157	22
Avg. Yards	4.0	1.7
Touchdowns	0	0

KICKOFF RETURNS		
Returns	46	59
Yards	1,241	1,276
Avg. Yards	27.0	21.6
Touchdowns	4	0
INTERCEPTION RETURNS		
Interceptions	26	27
Yards	284	370
Avg. Yards	10.9	13.7
Touchdowns	2	3
PENALTIES		
Penalties	48	55
Yards	531	482
FUMBLES		
Fumbles	19	23
Fumbles lost	10	14
SCORING		
Points	334	209
XP attempted	39	24
XP made	39	23
FG attempted	29	28
FG made	19	14
Pct. FG made	65.5	50.0
Safeties	1	0

STARTING LINEUPS

DALLAS COWBOYS

OFFENSE

Bob Hayes   SE
Tony Liscio   LT

ICE BOWL '67

John Niland	LG
Mike Connelly	C
Leon Donohue	RG
Ralph Neely	RT
Pettis Norman	TE
Lance Rentzel	FL
Don Meredith	QB
Dan Reeves	HB
Don Perkins	FB

DEFENSE

George Andrie	RDE
Bob Lilly	RDT
Jethro Pugh	LDT
Willie Townes	LDE
Chuck Howley	LLB
Lee Roy Jordan	MLB
Dave Edwards	RLB
Mike Johnson	RCB
Cornell Green	LCB
Mike Gaechter	SS
Mel Renfro	FS

GREEN BAY PACKERS

OFFENSE

Boyd Dowler	SE
Bob Skoronski	LT
Gale Gillingham	LG
Ken Bowman	C
Jerry Kramer	RG
Forrest Gregg	RT
Marv Fleming	TE
Carroll Dale	FL
Bart Starr	QB
Donny Anderson	HB
Chuck Mercein	FB

DEFENSE

Lionel Aldridge	RDE
Henry Jordan	RDT
Ron Kostelnik	LDT
Willie Davis	LDE
Dave Robinson	LLB
Ray Nitschke	MLB
Lee Roy Caffey	RLB
Bob Jeter	RCB
Herb Adderley	LCB
Tom Brown	SS
Willie Wood	FS

PLAY BY PLAY

FIRST QUARTER

Cowboys win coin toss, elect to receive.
Chandler kicks off to Stokes on the 5, returned to the 33.

DALLAS

1-10	DAL 33	Meredith pass complete to Hayes for 10
1-10	DAL 43	Reeves runs for 4
2-6	DAL 47	Meredith pass incomplete for Rentzel
3-6	DAL 47	Reeves runs for no gain
4-6	DAL 47	Villanueva punts to Wood on the 14, returned to the 18

GREEN BAY (12:54)

1-10	GB 18	Anderson runs for 5, fumbles; Mercein recovered
2-5	GB 23	Anderson runs for 4
3-1	GB 27	Anderson runs for 4
1-10	GB 31	Starr sacked for loss of 9
2-19	GB 22	Starr pass complete to Fleming; Dallas penalized for pass interference
1-10	GB 31	Starr pass complete to Anderson on left sideline for 17

ICE BOWL '67

1-10	GB 48	Anderson runs for 3
2-7	DAL 49	Mercein runs for 2
3-5	DAL 47	Starr pass incomplete for Anderson; Dallas penalized five yards for holding
1-10	DAL 42	Anderson runs for loss of 2
2-12	DAL 44	Mercein runs for 3
3-9	DAL 41	Starr pass complete to Dale for 17
1-10	DAL 24	Starr pass incomplete for Dowler
2-10	DAL 24	Starr pass complete to Dale for 15
1-9	DAL 9	Anderson runs for 1
2-8	DAL 8	Starr pass complete to Dowler in end zone, touchdown

Chandler kicks extra point
Packers 7, Cowboys 0
Chandler kicks off to Dallas 12 where it goes out of bounds after touching Stephens.

DALLAS (6:02)

1-10	DAL 12	Perkins runs for 5
2-5	DAL 17	Meredith pass complete to Hayes for 5
1-10	DAL 22	Perkins runs for 3
2-7	DAL 25	Perkins runs for 3
3-4	DAL 28	Perkins runs for 5
1-10	DAL 33	Meredith pass incomplete for Reeves
2-10	DAL 33	Perkins runs for no gain
3-10	DAL 33	Meredith pass incompletefor Rentzel
4-10	DAL 33	Villanueva punts to Wood; fair catch at Green Bay 34

GREEN BAY (1:57)

1-10	GB 43	Mercein runs for no gain
2-10	GB 34	Starr pass incomplete for Dale
3-10	GB 34	Starr pass to Mercein for 3
4-7	GB 37	Anderson punts to Rentzel; fair catch at Dallas 31

DALLAS (0:19)

1-10	DAL 31	Perkins runs for no gain

End of first quarter, Packers 7, Cowboys 0

SECOND QUARTER

DALLAS

2-10	DAL 31	Meredith pass incomplete for Rentzel
3-10	DAL 31	Meredith pass incomplete for Reeves
4-10	DAL 31	Villanueva punts to Green Bay 35, ball downed.

GREEN BAY (14:40)

1-10	GB 35	Wilson runs for 13
1-10	GB 48	Williams runs for 7
2-3	DAL 45	Williams runs for 2
3-1	DAL 43	Starr passes to Dowler for 43, touchdown

Chandler kicks extra point
Packers 14, Cowboys 0
Chandler kicks off to Stephens at 25, returned to Dallas 40

DALLAS (12:18)

1-10	DAL 40	Meredith pass for Hayes incomplete
2-10	DAL 40	Perkins runs for no gain
3-10	DAL 40	Meredith pass intercepted by Adderley at Dallas 47, returned 15 yards

GREEN BAY (11:20)

1-10	DAL 31	Wilson runs for no gain
2-10	DAL 31	Starr pass knocked down
3-10	DAL 31	Starr sacked for loss of 10
4-10	DAL 41	Anderson punts to Dallas 9; ball downed by Green Bay

DALLAS (10:19)

1-10	DAL 9	Perkins runs for 1
2-9	DAL 10	Perkins runs for 6
3-3	DAL 16	Reeves runs for loss of 2
4-5	DAL 14	Villanueva punts to Dallas 48; Brown loss of 2 on return

ICE BOWL '67

GREEN BAY (8:11)

1-10	DAL 50	Starr pass to Williams for 4
2-6	DAL 46	Wilson runs for loss of 2
3-8	DAL 48	Starr pass incomplete for Wilson
4-8	DAL 48	Anderson punts to Dallas 3; ball downed

DALLAS (4:09)

1-10	DAL 32	Baynham runs for loss of 1
2-11	DAL 31	Perkins runs for 4
3-7	DAL 34	Meredith pass to Hayes for 1
4-6	DAL 35	Villanueva punts to Wood on Green Bay 21; returned 10 yards

GREEN BAY (4:30)

1-10	GB 31	Packers penalized 5 yards for illegal procedure
1-15	GB 26	Starr sacked and fumbles; Andrie returned fumble 7 yards, touchdown

Villanueva kicks extra point
Packers 14, Cowboys 7
Villanueva kicks off into Green Bay end zone; no return

GREEN BAY (3:39)

1-10	GB 20	Williams runs for 1
2-9	GB 21	Starr pass incomplete for Wilson
3-9	GB 21	Cowboys penalized 5 yards for illegal procedure
3-4	GB 26	Starr sacked for loss of 5
4-9	GB 21	Anderson punts to Hayes; fair catch at Green Bay 47

DALLAS (2:30)

1-10	GB 47	Reeves runs for 2
2-8	GB 45	Clarke runs for loss of 8
3-16	DAL 47	Meredith pass incomplete for Rentzel
4-16	DAL 47	Villanueva punts to Wood; fair catch fumbled at 17; Clarke recovered for Dallas

DALLAS (1:34)

1-10	GB 17	Perkins runs for 3 (Nitschke)
2-7	GB 14	Meredith pass incomplete for Rentzel
3-7	GB 14	Meredith pass to Reeves for 1
4-6	GB 13	Villanueva kicks 21-yard field goal

Packers 14, Cowboys 10
Villanueva kicks to Weatherwax at Green Bay 41, 4-yard return

GREEN BAY (0:33)

| 1-10 | GB 45 | Starr pass knocked down by Lilly |
| 2-10 | GB 45 | Williams runs for 3 |

End of first half, Packers 14, Cowboys 10

THIRD QUARTER

Villanueva kicks off to Caffey on Green Bay 37, returned to 44

GREEN BAY (14:53)

1-10	GB 44	Anderson runs for 3
2-7	GB 47	Starr sacked for loss of 4
3-11	GB 43	Starr pass incomplete for Dowler
4-11	GB 43	Anderson punts to Rentzel; fair catch fumbled at 21; Clarke recovered at 11

DALLAS (12:48)

1-10	DAL 11	Meredith pass to Reeves for 7
2-3	DAL 18	Perkins runs for 8
1-10	DAL 26	Meredith pass incomplete for Reeves
2-10	DAL 26	Meredith pass to Clarke for 14
1-10	DAL 40	Reeves runs for 8
2-2	DAL 48	Reeves runs for 20
1-10	GB 32	Reeves runs for 3
2-7	GB 29	Meredith pass to Rentzel for 11
1-10	GB 18	Reeves runs for loss of 4
2-14	GB 22	Meredith pass incomplete for Rentzel
3-14	GB 22	Meredith runs for 9 and fumbles; Adderley recovers at Green Bay 13

ICE BOWL '67

GREEN BAY (7:51)

1-10	GB 13	Anderson runs for 1
2-9	GB 14	Anderson runs for 1
3-8	GB 15	Starr pass to Dale for 12
1-10	GB 27	Starr sacked for loss of 16
2-26	GB 11	Anderson runs for 6
3-20	GB 17	Anderson runs for 9
4-11	GB 26	Anderson punts to Rentzel; fair catch fumbled at 49, recovered at 46

DALLAS (4:48)

1-10	GB 46	Reeves runs for 11
1-10	GB 35	Meredith pass to Reeves for 3
2-7	GB 32	Reeves runs for 2
3-5	GB 30	Meredith sacked for loss of 9
4-14	GB 39	Villanueva misses 47-yard field goal attempt; Wood returns from 4 to the 27

GREEN BAY (2:00)

1-10	GB 27	Anderson runs for 5
2-5	GB 32	Anderson runs for 1
3-4	GB 33	Starr sacked for loss of 8
4-12	GB 41	Anderson punts to Dallas 45; Hayes makes fair catch

DALLAS (0:12)

1-10	DAL 45	Perkins runs for 5

End of third quarter, Packers 14, Cowboys 10

FOURTH QUARTER

DALLAS

2-5	50	Reeves option pass to Rentzel for 50 yards, touchdown

Villianueva kicks extra point

Cowboys 17, Packers 14

Villanueva kicks off to Crutcher on Green Bay 31, returned to 34

GREEN BAY (14:43)

1-10	GB 34	Starr pass incomplete; Cowboys penalized for pass interference
1-10	GB 48	Mercein runs for no gain
2-10	GB 48	Starr sacked for loss of 5
3-15	GB 43	Starr pass knocked down by Jordan
4-15	GB 43	Anderson punts to Dallas 19; ball downed

DALLAS (13:08)

1-10	DAL 19	Perkins runs for 1
2-9	DAL 20	Reeves runs for loss of 2 (Jordan, Davis)
3-11	DAL 18	Meredith pass incomplete for Hayes
4-11	DAL 18	Villanueva punts to Wood on Green Bay 30; Cowboys penalized for grabbing his facemask

GREEN BAY (11:18)

1-10	GB 47	Starr pass to Dowler for 19
1-10	DAL 34	Anderson runs for 1
2-9	DAL 33	Starr pass knocked down by Howley
3-9	DAL 33	Starr pass incomplete for Anderson
4-9	DAL 33	Chandler misses 40-yard field goal attempt

DALLAS (9:44)

1-10	DAL 20	Perkins runs for 5
2-5	DAL 25	Perkins runs for 1 (Kostelnik)
3-4	DAL 26	Perkins runs for 2; Packers penalized 5 yards for being offside
1-10	DAL 31	Reeves runs for 5
2-5	DAL 36	Reeves runs for loss of 5
3-10	DAL 31	Meredith pass to Clarke for 16
1-10	DAL 47	Perkins runs for no gain
2-10	DAL 47	Meredith pass to Baynham for loss of 3
3-13	DAL 44	Meredith pass incomplete for Rentzel
4-14	DAL 44	Villanueva punts to Wood on Green Bay 23, returned to 32

ICE BOWL '67

GREEN BAY (4:54)

1-10	GB 32	Starr pass to Anderson for 6
2-4	GB 38	Mercein runs for 7
1-10	GB 45	Starr pass to Dowler for 13
1-10	DAL 42	Anderson runs for loss of 9
2-19	GB 49	Starr pass to Anderson for 12
3-7	DAL 39	Starr pass to Anderson for 9
1-10	DAL 30	Starr pass to Mercein for 19
1-10	DAL 11	Mercein runs for 8
2-2	DAL 3	Anderson runs for 2
1-1	DAL 1	Anderson runs for no gain
2-1	DAL 1	Anderson runs for no gain
3-1	DAL 1	Starr QB sneak for 1 yard, touchdown

Chandler kicks extra point
Packers 21, Cowboys 17
Chandler kicks off to end zone, no return

DALLAS (0:13)

| 1-10 | DAL 20 | Meredith pass incomplete for Rentzel; Cowboys penalized 5 yards for illegal procedure |
| 1-15 | DAL 15 | Meredith pass incomplete to Hayes |

FINAL SCORE: PACKERS 21, COWBOYS 17

INDIVIDUAL AND TEAM STATISTICS

Green Bay   7 7 0 7 – 21
Dallas   0 10 0 7 – 17
GB: Dowler 8 pass from Starr (Chandler kick)
GB: Dowler 43 pass from Starr (Chandler kick)
DAL: Andrie 7 fumble return (Villanueva kick)
DAL: Villanueva 21-yard field goal
DAL: Rentzel 50 pass from Reeves (Villanueva kick)
GB: Starr 1 run (Chandler kick)

TEAM STATISTICS

	Dallas	Green Bay
First Downs	11	18
By Rush	4	5
By Pass	6	10
By Penalty	1	3
Total Yards	192	195
Net Yards Rushing	92	80
Net Yards Passing	100	115
Passing-Comp.-Att	11-26	14-24
Passing-Yards Per Att.	3.8	4.8
Fumbles-Lost	3-1	3-2
Penalties-Yards	7-58	2-10
Punts-Avg.	8-39.1	8-28.8

INDIVIDUAL STATISTICS

Rushing
Dallas: Perkins 17-51, Reeves 13-42, Meredith 1-9, Baynham 1-(-2), Clarke 1-(-8)
Green Bay: Anderson 18-35, Mercein 6-20, Williams 4-13, Wilson 3-11, Starr 1-1

Passing
Dallas: Meredith 10-25-59-1 Int; Reeves 1-1-50, 1 TD
Green Bay: Starr 14-24-191-2 TDs

Receiving
Dallas: Hayes 3-16, Reeves 3-11, Rentzel 2-61 TD, Clarke 2-24, Baynham 1-(-3)
Green Bay: Dowler 4-77 2 TDs, Anderson 4-44, Dale 3-44, Mercein 2-22, Williams 1-4

PACKERS THROUGH THE YEARS

OFFENSE

Bart Starr, QB: Played for Packers from 1956 to 1971; two-time Super Bowl champ; two-time Super Bowl MVP; five-time NFL champ; four-time Pro Bowl; NFL MVP 1966; member of NFL All-1960s Decade team; inducted into Pro Football Hall of Fame in 1977; Packers head coach from 1975 to 1983; No. 15 retired by Packers; suffered several health setbacks in recent years but was on hand for Brett Favre's Hall of Fame induction in 2015; still lives in Alabama with his wife, Cherry.

Donny Anderson, HB: First-round Packer draft pick in 1965; played for Packers through 1971; traded to St. Louis Cardinals in 1972 and played three seasons; rushed for 3,165 yards and 24 touchdowns and caught 125 passes in six seasons with Packers; averaged 39.6 yards on 315 punts with Packers; retired in 1975; Pro Bowler in 1968; member of Packers Hall of Fame; lives in Dallas, Texas.

Chuck Mercein, FB: Played part of three seasons for Packers; drafted in third round by New York Giants in 1965; signed by Packers late in 1967 season by Lombardi for insurance purposes; played one snap in Super Bowl II after earning "hero" status in the Ice Bowl; completed career with New York Jets and retired in 1971; went on to successful business career and is now a motivational speaker who revels in talking about Ice Bowl.

Boyd Dowler, SE: Packers third-round draft pick in 1959; played in Green Bay for 11 seasons, catching 448 passes for 6,918 yards and 40 touchdowns; played one season in Washington in 1971 before retiring; his 448 receptions is still sixth all-time in team history; Rookie of the Year in 1959; two-time Pro Bowl; a member of 1960s NFL All-Decade Team and the NFL 50th anniversary team; inducted into Packers Hall of Fame in 1978; after retirement was assistant coach for Rams, Eagles, Redskins, Bengals, and Buccaneers; now a scout for the Atlanta Falcons.

Carroll Dale, FL: Drafted by Los Angeles Rams in 1960; traded to Packers in 1965 for linebacker Dan Currie; played for Packers through 1972, catching 275 passes, averaging nearly 20 yards per catch and scoring 35 touchdowns; finished career in 1973 with Minnesota Vikings; resides in Virginia and still works in athletic department at University of Virginia.

Marv Fleming, TE: An 11th-round draft of Packers in 1963; played for Packers through 1969, catching 109 passes for 1,300 yards and 12 touchdowns; played for Miami Dolphins from 1970 to 1974; a five-time NFL champ (three with Packers, two with Dolphins) and four-time Super Bowl champ; inducted into Packers Hall of Fame in 2010; lives in Los Angeles working with local charities.

Bob Skoronski, LT: Fifth-round draft pick of Packers in 1956; started as a rookie then served two years in Air Force; returned in 1959 as a starter for first-year coach Vince Lombardi; called by many the most underrated Packer on those championship teams; made Pro Bowl in 1966; retired after 1968 season; inducted into Packers Hall of Fame in 1976; became successful in several businesses after football; splits time between Madison, Wisconsin, and Florida.

Gale Gillingham, LG: First-round draft pick of Packers in 1966; eventually replaced long-time left guard and fan favorite Fuzzy Thurston; six-time All-Pro; five-time Pro Bowl; two-time

Associated Press First Team All-Pro; played entire career with Packers before retiring after 1976 season; inducted into Packers Hall of Fame in 1982; went into real estate in his native Minnesota after retirement and retired in 2010; he died in 2011.

Ken Bowman, C: Was a key part of the double team with right guard Jerry Kramer on the block that opened the hole for Bart Starr to sneak in for the winning TD in the Ice Bowl; an eighth-round draft pick of the Packers in 1964 who played his college ball for the University of Wisconsin; played for Packers from 1964 to 1973; played one season in the old World Football League then retired in 1974; studied for the law in the offseason and became a lawyer after retiring; inducted into Packers Hall of Fame in 1981; lives in Oro Valley, Arizona, and still presides as a circuit court judge.

Jerry Kramer, RG: Still considered one of the great guards in NFL history and noted as the perhaps best player never to be inducted into Pro Football Hall of Fame; drafted by Packers in 1958; struggled under new head coach Vince Lombardi but soon became perhaps Lombardi's most eloquent and strongest defender; wrote best-selling book *Instant Replay* with Dick Schaap about 1967 season; kicked field goals and extra points early in his career; three-time Pro Bowl; five-time All-Pro; member of NFL's 1960s All-Decade Team and 50th anniversary team; inducted into Packers Hall of Fame in 1975; in retirement he lives in Idaho and has been involved in many business interests but has always made the Packers his ultimate business.

Forrest Gregg, RT: Called by Lombardi the best offensive linemen he ever coached; second-round pick of Packers in 1956; played for Packers through 1970 and was named to Pro Bowl nine times; seven-time All-Pro; member of NFL's 1960s All-Decade Team and the Packers 75th anniversary team; inducted into Packers Hall of Fame in 1977; upon retirement, went into coaching starting as offensive line coach of San Diego Chargers and Cleveland Browns; was head coach of Cleveland Browns (1975–77), Cincinnati Bengals (1980–83), and Green Bay Packers (1984–87); also head coach at his alma mater Southern Methodist (1989–90); retired and living in Colorado Springs, Colorado, where he reportedly is suffering with Parkinson's Disease.

DEFENSE

Willie Davis, DE: Originally a 15th-round draft pick of the Cleveland Browns in 1956, he was traded to the Packers in 1960 for A. D. Williams; five-time Pro Bowl; five-time All-Pro; second in team history with 21 recovered fumbles; inducted into the Pro Football Hall of Fame in 1981; member of Packers' 75th anniversary team; inducted into Packers Hall of Fame in 1975; after retirement, he earned his MBA from the University of Chicago and went on to run several successful businesses and was on the board of numerous companies; he is retired and living in Los Angeles.

Ron Kostelnik, DT: Considered by his teammates one of the more unheralded members of a dominant defense; drafted in the second round by the Packers in 1961, he became a starter in 1965; he played on all five NFL champions, including two Super Bowls; traded to the Baltimore Colts in 1969 and retired after one season; inducted into Packers Hall of Fame in 1989; he became a business distributor in Appleton, Wisconsin, after retirement and died of a heart attack in 1993 at age fifty-three.

Henry Jordan, DT: Originally a fifth-round draft pick of the Cleveland Browns in 1957, he was traded to the Packers in 1959 for a fourth-round draft pick—one of the first trades made by new coach Vince Lombardi; four-time Pro Bowl and seven-time All-Pro; member of Packers 75th anniversary team; retired after 1969 season and settled in Milwaukee where he ran the summer festival known as Summerfest; inducted into the Pro Football Hall of Fame in 1995; inducted into Packers Hall of Fame in 1975; died of a heart attack in 1977 at age forty-two.

Lionel Aldridge, DE: One of the few rookies to ever start for Vince Lombardi; a fourth-round draft pick of the Packers in 1963, he played on three championship teams; traded to the San Diego Chargers in 1972, he played two more seasons before retiring; inducted into Packers Hall of Fame in 1988; tried his hand at radio color analysis but was soon overwhelmed by paranoid schizophrenia that left him homeless for a time; he became a vocal advocate for mental health in the following years but died of congestive heart failure in 1998 at the age of fifty-six.

Dave Robinson, LLB: Green Bay's first-round draft choice in 1963, he became a full-time starter in 1965; recorded 21 interceptions in his years with the Packers; 1968 Pro Bowl Lineman of the Game; three-time Pro Bowl; three-time All-Pro; traded to Washington Redskins in 1973 and played there two seasons before retiring; went into numerous business ventures after retirement; inducted into Pro Football Hall of Fame in 2013; inducted into Packers Hall of Fame in 1982; lives in Akron, Ohio.

Ray Nitschke, MLB: Still considered one of the great middle linebackers in NFL history, especially in an era dominated by great middle linebackers such as Dick Butkus and Sam Huff; ferocious on the field, he was kind and bookish off the field and never lost his love for the Packers; third-round draft pick of Packers in 1958; member of the Packers 75th anniversary team and 1960s All-Decade; ranked by *Sporting News* as 18th great player of all time; his No. 66 was retired by Packers in 1983; retired in 1972 and remained in Green Bay; inducted into Pro Football Hall of Fame in 1978; inducted into Packers Hall of Fame in 1978; suffered heart attack in 1998 and died at age sixty-one.

Lee Roy Caffey, RLB: A seventh-round draft pick of the Philadelphia Eagles in 1963, he was traded to the Packers in 1964 for center Jim Ringo; started 80 of a possible 84 games for Green Bay and had perhaps the best game of any Packer defender in the Ice Bowl; Pro Bowl and All-Pro and a member of the Packers 75th anniversary team; inducted into Packers Hall of Fame in 1986; traded to Chicago Bears along with Bob Hyland and Elijah Pitts for second overall pick in 1970 draft; also played for Dallas Cowboys and San Diego Chargers before retiring after 1972 season; settled in his native Texas after retiring and died of cancer in 1994 at the age of fifty-two.

Herb Adderley, LCB: First African American first-round draft for the Packers in 1961; originally drafted as a running back, was moved to defensive back; in nine season with Packers, intercepted 39 passes, returning seven for touchdowns, second in Packers history; five-time Pro Bowl; four-time All-Pro; member of NFL 1960s All-Decade Team; traded to Dallas Cowboys in 1970 where he played in two more Super Bowls; traded in 1973 to Los Angeles Rams, he retired instead; inducted into Packers Hall of Fame in

1981; inducted into Pro Football Hall of Fame in 1980; did some television work after retirement and now lives in New Jersey.

Bob Jeter, RCB: Originally a second-round draft pick of the Packers in 1960, he instead played two seasons with British Columbia of the Canadian Football League; joined the Packers in 1963 and finished with 23 interceptions in eight seasons; teamed up with Herb Adderley to make up what many considered the best cornerback duo in football; two-time Pro Bowl; inducted into Packers Hall of Fame in 1985; traded to Chicago Bears in 1971 and retired after the 1973 season; remained in Chicago after retirement and worked with kids in the recreation department; died of a heart attack in 2008 at age seventy-one.

Tom Brown, SS: A second-round draft pick of the Packers in 1963, he was also a superb baseball player and spent time with the Washington Senators; joined the Packers in 1964 and his interception in the end zone at the Cotton Bowl sealed Green Bay's 1966 NFL title; finished with 13 career interceptions; traded to Washington Redskins in 1969, the first trade made by Vince Lombardi in his new role as general manager of the Redskins; he retired after the 1970 season due to injury; now lives in Salisbury, Maryland, and created the Tom Brown Rookie League for youth baseball players.

Willie Wood, FS: Signed as a free agent by the Packers in 1960, he requested a shift from quarterback to safety, where he became one of the best in the NFL history; eight-time Pro Bowl; five-time All-Pro; member of the 1960s NFL All-Decade Team; finished his career with 48 interceptions, still second-best in team history behind Bobby Dillon; inducted into Pro Football Hall of Fame in 1989; inducted into Packers Hall of Fame in 1977; retired after

1971 season and coached in the NFL, World Football League, and Canadian Football League; lives in his native Washington, DC, and is suffering from dementia.

DALLAS COWBOYS THROUGH THE YEARS

OFFENSE

Don Meredith, QB: Considered by many Cowboys fans the original Dallas Cowboys player and still one of its most popular; drafted in 1960 before the Cowboys had been awarded a franchise, Meredith was drafted by the Chicago Bears as a favor from George Halas who wanted the Cowboys to have a solid foundation; took over as starter in 1963 and threw for 17,199 yards and 135 touchdowns; played in two NFL title games and lost both to Packers; three-time Pro Bowl; NFL Player of the Year in 1966; retired unexpectedly before 1969 season to pursue career as an actor; gained fame as color analyst for *Monday Night Football;* earned spot in Cowboys Ring of Honor in 1976; died of stroke in 2010 at the age of seventy-two.

Dan Reeves, HB: Signed as free agent by Cowboys in 1965; started as a defensive back but moved to running back due to team injuries; rushed for 1,990 yards and 25 touchdowns and caught 129 passes; his 50-yard touchdown pass to Lance Rentzel was Cowboys' highlight in Ice Bowl; a knee injury in 1968 slowed his career and he became a player/coach for Cowboys; he retired in 1972 and became assistant coach for Cowboys from 1974 to 1980; head coach of Denver Broncos, New York Giants, and Denver Broncos; appeared in nine Super Bowls as a player or coach; now lives in Atlanta.

Don Perkins, FB: Like Don Meredith, was drafted too late for 1960 season so signed personal services contract with team owner Clint Murchison; missed rookie season with broken foot; named NFL Rookie of the Year in 1961; three-time All-Pro; six-time Pro Bowl; rushed for 6,217 yards, still third-best in team history; considered best fullback in team history; inducted in Cowboys Ring of Honor in 1976; retired after 1968 season and did radio and TV football analysis before becoming director of a work incentive program for the state of New Mexico; also involved in local theater and public speaking and is living in Albuquerque, New Mexico.

Lance Rentzel, FL: Originally a second-round draft pick of the Minnesota Vikings in 1965 as a running back; traded to Cowboys in 1967 for a third-round draft pick and Dallas converted him to flanker; caught dramatic 50-yard touchdown pass from Dan Reeves in Ice Bowl; led NFL in 1969 by averaging 22 yards per catch and 12 touchdown receptions; caught 183 passes for 3,521 yards and 31 touchdowns with Cowboys; off-field incidents of indecent exposure dogged his career and was traded to Los Angeles Rams in 1971; placed on waivers prior to 1975 season and retired; now lives in Dallas.

Bob Hayes, SE: The gold medalist in the 100 meter dash in the 1964 Olympics, Hayes was drafted by the Cowboys in the seventh round in 1964 without knowing if he had any real football ability; went on to become one of the great receivers in team history; still holds ten team receiving and four punt return records; caught 365 passes for 7,295 yards and 71 touchdowns for Cowboys; led league in punt return average in 1968; three-time Pro Bowl; two-time All-Pro; traded to San Francisco 49ers in 1975 but was waived by midseason; inducted into Pro Football Hall of Fame by senior committee in 2009; inducted into Cowboys Ring of Honor in in 2001; battled drug issues after retiring to Jacksonville, Florida; died in 2002 of kidney failure at age fifty-nine.

Pettis Norman, TE: Signed with Cowboys as an undrafted free agent in 1962; began as a wide receiver but moved to tight end; split time at tight end when Cowboys acquired Mike Ditka in 1969; caught 124 passes for 1,672 yards and 14 touchdowns in his nine seasons with Cowboys; traded to the San Diego Chargers in 1971 and retired in 1973; active in civil rights movement as a player and after he retired; became successful businessman in Dallas and still lives there.

Tony Liscio, LT: Drafted in third round by Green Bay Packers in 1963 but was waived the week before the season opener; picked up off waivers by Dallas Cowboys where he earned a reputation as one of the most reliable offensive linemen in team history; missed entire 1965 season with injury; traded to San Diego Chargers in spring of 1971 but did not play due to injury; traded to Miami Dolphins in the fall of 1971 but injuries forced him to retire; due to injuries to other linemen in November of '71, Liscio was recruited by Tom Landry to return to the field; despite leg injuries, he played eight games, including the Cowboys' win in the Super Bowl; retired for good after that; ran successful real estate business in Dallas after retirement and still lives there.

John Niland, LG: Drafted by the Dallas Cowboys in the first round in 1966, the first time the Cowboys had taken an offensive linemen in the first round; six-time Pro Bowl; three-time All-Pro;

considered one of the great offensive linemen of the era; traded to Philadelphia Eagles in 1975; retired in 1976 and continues to live in Dallas area where's a motivational speaker.

Mike Connelly, C: Drafted by the Los Angeles Rams in the 12th round in 1959; released in 1960 and picked up by Cowboys; considered the strongest man on the team; lost starting job to Dave Manders in 1965 but reclaimed it 1967 when Manders was injured; at the start of 1968 training camp, he told Landry he would play just one season and he was traded the next day to Pittsburgh Steelers for kicker Mike Clark; he did in fact retire after 1968 season; after retirement he built homes for disadvantaged in Dallas area and still lives there.

Leon Donohue, RG: Originally drafted by the San Francisco 49ers in the ninth round in 1961, a year ahead of when he was scheduled to graduate from college; traded to Cowboys in 1965 where he started at right guard for three seasons; a knee injury ended his 1968 season; traded in 1969 to the Detroit Lions but his knee injury forced him to retire; after leaving football, he became football, softball, and wrestling coach at Shasta College in California; eventually took over as head football coach and retired in 1995; died in 2016 at age seventy-seven.

Ralph Neely, RT: Along with Packers guard Jerry Kramer, considered one the greatest players never to be elected to the Pro Football Hall of Fame; drafted by Baltimore Colts in the second round in 1965; rights traded to Dallas Cowboys for punter Billy Lothridge and a fourth-round draft pick; manned Cowboys offensive line for 13 seasons as both a right tackle and left tackle; four-time All-Pro; two-time Pro Bowl; member of the NFL

All-Rookie team in 1965; member of the NFL 1960s All-Decade Team; retired in 1977.

DEFENSE

Willie Townes, LDE: Drafted by the Cowboys in the second round in 1966; unofficially credited with nine quarterback sacks in 1966, tying him for all-time Cowboys record; his sack of Bart Starr and the resulting fumble led to a change in momentum in Ice Bowl; missed half of 1968 season and all of '69 season with hamstring injury; traded to New Orleans Saints in 1970 and released in 1971.

Jethro Pugh, LDT: Drafted by the Cowboys in the 11th round in 1965; went on to play 14 seasons with the Cowboys, one of the longest stints in team history; amassed an unofficial 95.5 quarterback sacks and was the team leader from 1968 to 1972; Kramer and Bowman's block on him in the Ice Bowl was what allowed Starr to sneak into the end zone and it bothered Pugh for years afterward; retired after 1978 season Super Bowl XIII when the Cowboys lost to the Steelers; after retirement was involved with United Negro College Fund and ran a string of Western-themed gift shops at the Dallas-Fort Worth airport; died in 2015 of natural causes at age seventy.

Bob Lilly, RDT: One of the great Dallas Cowboys of all time and nicknamed "Mr. Cowboy"; drafted in the first round by the Cowboys in 1961; at one stage played in 196 straight games; 11-time Pro Bowl; seven-time All-Pro; member of the NFL's 1960s and '70s All-Decade Teams as well as the NFL 75th anniversary team; first Cowboys player enshrined in the team's Ring of Honor in

1975; inducted into Pro Football Hall of Fame in 1980; listed 10th in the *Sporting News'* 100 Greatest Football Players of All Time; his No. 74 has not been worn another Cowboys' player since his retirement in 1975 except by Lawrence Okoye in the 2016 preseason; after retirement he has been involved with various businesses though photography and art are his passions; now lives in Georgetown, Texas.

George Andrie, RDE: Drafted by Cowboys in the sixth round in 1962; played all 11 pro seasons with Cowboys, starting 112 straight regular-season games at one stage; NFL All-Rookie Team; one-time All-Pro; five-time Pro Bowl; unofficially registered 97 career quarterback sacks and was team leader from 1964 to 1967; his fumble return for a touchdown in Ice Bowl changed the game's momentum; retired in 1972; runs George Andrie and Associates, a promotional products company in Waco, Texas.

Chuck Howley, LLB: Originally a first-round draft pick by the Chicago Bears in 1958, he sustained a serious knee injury in 1959 and retired; after missing 1960 season, he attempted a comeback and his rights were traded to the Cowboys for two picks in the '63 draft; went on to be one of the great linebackers in team history; six-time Pro Bowl; five-time All-Pro; Super Bowl V MVP; intercepted 25 passes and recovered 18 fumbles; enshrined in Cowboys' Ring of Honor in 1977; retired in 1973 and now raises quarter horses in Dallas area.

Lee Roy Jordan, MLB: Selected by the Cowboys in the first round of the 1963, another key piece in what would come to be known as the "Doomsday Defense"; finished his career with 743 solo tackles, which is still second in team history; intercepted

36 passes and recovered 18 fumbles; five-time Pro Bowl; named All-Pro once; enshrined in the Cowboys Ring of Honor in 1989; retired in 1976 after playing his entire career with the Cowboys; runs a lumber company in the Dallas area.

Dave Edwards, RLB: Originally drafted by the Denver Broncos of the AFL, he decided instead to sign as a free agent with the Cowboys; along with Chuck Howley and Lee Roy Jordan, formed perhaps the most dominant linebacking corps in the NFL for a decade; in final 11 seasons, missed only one game due to injury; intercepted 13 passes and recovered 17 fumbles; after retiring in 1975, he turned to a career as an artistic painter; died in his sleep at home in December 2016 at the age of seventy-six as he was preparing for heart surgery the following week.

Cornell Green, LCB: A standout basketball player at Utah State who had never played football, he signed as a free agent with the Cowboys in 1962; named to NFL All-Rookie team that season; five-time Pro Bowl; four-time All-Pro; named to Cowboys 25th anniversary team; never missed a game in 13-year career (182 games); intercepted 34 passes; retired in 1974 and became a scout for the Cowboys; later scouted for Denver Broncos and retired in 2015.

Mike Johnson, RCB: Drafted by the Oakland Raiders in 1966, he instead signed as a free agent with the Cowboys; played in same backfield at Kansas University with Gale Sayers; Cowboys moved him to defensive back; best season was 1967 when he took over cornerback spot from Warren Livingston and posted five interceptions; lost starting job in 1969; traded to Chicago Bears in 1970 but never appeared in another NFL game.

Mike Gaechter, SS: One of the hardest hitters in team history; signed as a free agent by Cowboys in 1962 and soon became mainstay in defensive backfield; still owns record for two of the longest interception returns for TDs in team history (100 yards in 1962 and 86 yards in 1963); intercepted 21 passes in his career; ruptured his Achilles tendon in 1969 and missed all of the 1970 season; traded to Washington Redskins in 1971 but was released; he sued the Cowboys twice for medical malpractice over the years; developed Alzheimer's and died in August 2015 of heart failure at age seventy-five.

Mel Renfro, FS: One of the great defensive backs in team history; second-round draft choice of the Cowboys in 1964; ten-time Pro Bowl; five-time All-Pro; intercepted 52 passes which remains a team record; his 14 seasons with Cowboys is second all-time in length of service; also a quality punt and kickoff returner; inducted into Pro Football Hall of Fame in 1996; enshrined in Cowboys' Ring of Honor in 1981; retired in 1977 and was an assistant coach first in the USFL and then with the St. Louis Cardinals; lives in Dallas area and is a motivational speaker.

Index